the JOURNEY after LIFE

the JOURNEY after LIFE

What Happens When We Die

cyndi dale

SOUNDS TRUE
BOULDER, COLORADO

Sounds True, Inc.
Boulder CO 80306

Published 2013

Previously published in hardcover as *Illuminating the Afterlife*

Book design by Karen Polaski

Printed in the United States of America

Library of Congress Cataloging-in-Publication Data
Dale, Cyndi.
  The journey after life : what happens when we die / Cyndi Dale.
     pages cm
  Includes bibliographical references and index.
  ISBN 978-1-60407-853-4
  1. Death. 2. Future life. 3. Parapsychology. 4. Occultism. I. Title.
  BF1999.D1555 2013
  133.901'3--dc23
                              2013022065

Lyrics from Norman Greenbaum's "Spirit in the Sky," reprinted by permission of
Great Honesty Music. "There Were Songs My Mother Never Got to Sing" and
"Time Is the River" used by permission of the poems' author, Roger Cooper.

10 9 8 7 6 5 4 3 2

Ebook ISBN: 978-1-62203-069-9

To my mother,

Solveig Norstog,

who has kept faith with me through my entire life.

Time
Is the river
In which
All is . . .

ROGER COOPER

CONTENTS

CONTENTS

ACKNOWLEDGMENTS

First and foremost a thank-you to Jo Ann Deck, whose ideas and dreams of heaven initiated this book, and also to Karine and Karen of Earth Futures in Russia, whose persistent request for a book about the afterlife finally made me sit down and write it.

More than a thank-you—an awed bow—to Sounds True founder, Tami Simon, who has established a company illuminated with the integrity she herself displays, a standard equally illustrated by Jennifer Coffee, whose belief in this book invited it into being. Cathy Scofield was an invaluable first editor, even driving to Boulder to hear my "wild ideas," while Sheridan McCarthy, freelance editor, pulled information from my depths, creating a book that truly reflects the beauty and hopefulness of the topic. Another huge thank-you to Randy Roark of Sounds True, whose production savvy created the audio version of the Planes, and an additional blessing to Kelly Notaras, editorial director at Sounds True, who has shaped the book into something I am proud of.

Of course, there has been the critical participation of my children: Gabriel, whose wit and wisdom punctuate my writing—and whose incessant chatter prompts me to finish my projects quickly and succinctly. There's my son Michael, whose solid acceptance of death through the years has encouraged my own desire to fearlessly embrace the topic. And there is Katie, my special daughter, whose newborn son reminded me that while souls are exiting, there are always shining ones entering.

And nothing would have come of the book without my business manager and agent extraordinaire, Anthony J. Benson, who found a home for the book, spurred me into action, and provided inspiration and encouragement throughout the process.

Finally, a blessing to everyone—to all of us—affected by the bombing of the World Trade Center in New York on that fateful September 11. The legacy of our sacrifice reminds us that, in the end, our task is to continually choose peace, forgiveness, and love. This is the true wisdom of the Planes of Light.

INTRODUCTION

*Someone who dies before he dies does not die
when he dies.*

HOLGER KALWEIT
DREAMTIME & INNER SPACE

What is this invisible landscape called death? Is it the cessation of life as we know it? The beginning of new worlds? Is this experience the same for each of us, or is it unique to our own personalities and characteristics? What possible purpose could there be in such an unknown and unknowable adventure? And what is this veil of not knowing? Why do we fear this thing that we do not know? Is it possible to dispel the clouds and illuminate the subject and the process we call "death"?

As an energy healer and intuitive counselor, and as a person with many loved ones, I am always aware of death. Clients frequently come to me seeking healing, and sometimes to stave off death. Some come to recover from someone else's death. Others want to learn how to live. My role in every case is the same. I help people to know life and death as identical things, and to fully embrace both.

Most of us are curious about what really happens when we die, but we aren't satisfied by the answers we find on TV, in books or magazines, or even in religion classes. There is no conclusive evidence, no certainty, of a life after death. But it is also true that there is nothing certain in life, either. You might apply for a job, but that doesn't mean you will get it. You could become pregnant, but that doesn't mean you will bear a child. You can get out of your bed in the morning, but there is no guarantee that you will return to it that night.

We live on the faith that there will be a tomorrow. And when we are done with tomorrows, we would like to believe that there is something more.

There is.

The Planes of Light.

I am psychic. I was raised in a "normal" family, one that worshipped in the Lutheran Church on Sundays. Psychics were not accepted in a normal world like this. I saw colors around people, which I have come to learn are the chakras and auric fields, energy bands that manage and explain our personalities. I heard ghosts, often awakening in the night to converse with the various deceased people who walked around in our house.

My parents were surprised, and disconcerted, when I knew that one of my grandmothers had died before they told me; she had already visited me, saying her good-byes. I had tea parties with angels, their great white wings dipping into my invisible tea and knocking over the real-life sugar cookies. And I lay awake at night listening to the singing of the wind faeries.

As my parents tried to discourage me from being "overimaginative," I began to wonder why I could see and hear things that they could not. And, as children often do, I decided that it must be because there was something wrong with me. I did my best to inhibit my curiosity, to close down. But then I attended my first funeral.

I was in third grade, and it was the funeral of my parents' friend Jean. Her body lay in an open casket. She wore a light blue suit and a lot of makeup. I thought she looked awfully still, so I touched her cheek to see if she would respond. She didn't move, and I started to cry. There was no one in this body!

"She's dead, Cyndi," my mother whispered. I asked what that meant. "She has gone to heaven to live with God."

"What is she doing in heaven?" I asked. I had always had many questions; maybe this was the time to get some answers.

"She is singing with the angels," my mother explained, seeming satisfied with her answer.

Two thoughts crossed my mind. First, if heaven was all about angels singing, I was not sure I wanted to go there. As a blue-eyed blonde, I was always chosen to represent the angelic realm in plays at school and church. I hated to sing, and I hated angel costumes. Ultimately, being good seemed boring to me, and I thought that if

Jean and everyone else were going to go to heaven, I would prefer to go to the other place I'd heard about.

The second thought was that my mother had not been correctly informed as to Jean's whereabouts. Jean was certainly not lying in the coffin—that body was empty—but neither was she floating around in some remote heaven. In fact, I could see her in the pastor's pulpit!

This was the real Jean, and she looked younger than the artificial Jean in the coffin. Without the horrible, yellowish makeup she appeared vibrant. She was barefoot and looking comfortable in an ethereal spring-green dress. I could hear her faintly; she seemed to be delivering her own sermon, about love and forgiveness. Every so often she would wave her hand and golden light would spill out, float to the floor, and swirl around the feet of those gathered to mark her passing. I wanted to talk to her and began moving toward the pulpit, but my mother dragged me back to my seat.

After the funeral I started to learn everything I could about death. I conducted in-depth conversations with some of the ghosts in the house. I read the Bible—three times, in fact, before the fifth grade—trying to find out what really happens to us when we die. It was full of stories about the afterlife, spirits, and psychic visitations. In Sunday school I learned that Ezekiel was taken up into the heavens, and so was the Apostle Paul. Elijah ascended—without dying. Jesus rose from the dead. Saul talked to a dead spirit, Joseph received dreams and did divination, and Samuel prayed and was answered by angels. Mary was instructed by an angel. People healed one another through prayer and the laying on of hands.

The notion of a single heaven and a coming Judgment Day just didn't make sense to me. I was certain that I was not being told the truth about the worlds inhabited by spirits, and other aspects of death.

Since those early years, I've had countless experiences with spirits and the world of the afterlife. I have met people who have had near-death experiences and lived to tell about them. In client sessions, I have been honored to receive images or words from souls who have died to pass along to loved ones. In this book, I want to offer the fruit of all my experiences and continued research and describe to you the after-death life.

The Planes of Light: The Worlds After This

I started working on this book several years ago. It was September 8, 2001, and I was flying from Minneapolis to Phoenix. I had just settled in to read a long-awaited novel, when a voice spoke to me.

"I want you to write a book about life after death," it said. "I will reveal what you need to know."

I was both surprised and scared. Despite my lifetime interest in death and dying, I didn't consider myself an expert. While other intuitives readily "channeled the dead," for me it was a less-frequent occurrence. What would I find out? Would I do the information justice?

Swallowing my reaction, I put my book aside and began to write. I scribbled down everything that came in my head, and over the next few days I received several visions describing the dying process, the worlds after death, and details about dying, the afterlife, and returning to life. The information was fascinating, but it did not begin to have a personal impact until three days later.

On September 11, 2001, terrorists destroyed the World Trade Center in New York City. Throughout the following year, I received psychic impressions of what happens at death, from the ways the soul separates from the body to descriptions of the interdimensional tunnels that operate as exit points. I was also told, intuitively and psychically, many stories of those who died that day. I watched as some souls were guided out of life and others remained behind as ghosts. I viewed the many levels of existence that were open to the departing souls, learning who went where — and why.

Since that time, I have asked my own spiritual guides to continue explaining what really happens at death and beyond. I have kept notes, and asked more questions. I have received the answers in dreams, visions, and audible messages. In client sessions I have received information from deceased souls that answers many questions, and my clients have told me their own experiences with loved ones who have died.

I have learned that we have nothing to fear from death but our own fear of it. In fact, I have learned that there is no death; there are only planes of light — gradient levels of awareness that invite our soul's evolution.

The Journey After Life is a description of the brilliant spaces and places of awareness that we each pass through in order to fully embrace our own luminescence. The purpose of this journey is soul evolution. Our souls are like children playing in the universe. They began as innocents, eager to touch and be touched, to grow and develop. Our souls emerged from our own spirits, which are the infinite and always-loving selves that remain connected to the Greater Spirit. The soul, however, does not want to sing endless angel songs in heaven. It wants experience. For this, it comes to life. And then, taking life's experience along, it learns more in the afterlife.

This book is a journey into and beyond death, describing what occurs physically, energetically, and spiritually while you are dying and what choices you face upon leaving your physical body. It also offers concrete ways to negotiate the soul's evolutionary path while alive.

Practicing Death: The True Purpose of This Book

It is said that when Plato was on his deathbed he proclaimed that life's most important task was to "practice to die."[1] To the Greeks, death meant *lysis* and *chorismos,* or loosening and separating. Through Plato's eyes, therefore, death would simply be the physical and energetic loosening from life, a separation from what he had believed to be real.

Seen in this way, life is the readying for the adventure that we term *death.*

Cultures long before and since Plato have examined death through a discipline often called *thanatology,* the study of the medical, psychological, and sociological aspects of death. But death is not only something that can be researched, dissected, or mentally scrutinized. It is something to be felt. For just as my death is personal to me, so is your death personal to you. They will be different experiences. And we can prepare for them now.

What You Will Learn

In this book, I will offer insights into several topics that are related to an understanding of death. I will examine issues such as:

- Definitions of the parts of the self, including body, mind, soul, and spirit
- Aspects of soul healing, including recession, possession, and fragmentation
- The types of spirits and other entities that have an impact on death, including angels of death, demons, and the masters of the Planes of Light
- Questions of heaven, hell, and purgatory
- Violent death situations, such as sudden death, suicide, genocide, and torture
- The impact of abortion, adoption, and other birth issues
- Other circumstances of dying and what they mean, including illnesses and conditions such as Alzheimer's disease

When it is time for us to transcend the earth, we prepare for death—for the voyage from darkness to light. There are many stages of death and dying. I will describe these in energetic terms, discussing the various ways the body, mind, and soul prepare for death, and why. I will share brief discourses on the different ways we die and what each might mean for the developing soul, and then relate the steps the body goes through as the soul prepares to leave. I will also examine the birthing process, showing the circular nature of our progression from life to death, and back again.

Some of my descriptions will involve energy-related terms that might be new to you—including words like *chakra, energy body,* and *auric field.* Fundamentally, we are all made of energy, which can be defined as *information that moves.* Energy cannot be destroyed; it can merely change form. Therefore, none of us can be destroyed—we can only transform. In order to explain the metamorphosis you will go through at and after death, I discuss what happens energetically, and to help you understand this process, I will include definitions of these concepts.

I will describe the actual process of soul separation. Death is nothing more than the separation and transition of the soul from a dense physical state to a higher vibrational state. In order for the soul to release its density, which it took on at birth, it must increase vibration. There are a variety of vibratory tunnels that accomplish this goal. Each of these tunnels spins at a different frequency and ends at a different location. Depending upon its goals and needs, a soul exits the body through one of these tunnels.

I will explain these vibratory tunnels and where they lead. I will also discuss the various reasons that a soul might select one tunnel over another—or bypass this process altogether. I'll explore the very interesting ideas of ghosts, ghouls, vampires, and phantoms, as well as concepts such as reincarnation. I will also look at some of the other entities, energies, and spirits that inhabit this and other worlds.

Finally, I will invite you to investigate the Planes of Light, the spectrum of higher dimensions that vibrate at higher frequencies than the earth plane. Each of these Planes represents a different truth or body of higher knowledge. Each is managed by a different set of masters, which greet the incoming soul and guide it through that realm. In addition, each requires a certain set of criteria in order for the soul to "graduate" and move to the next level. Just as you experienced in the schools you have attended during your life, there are challenges on these Planes. I will discuss the difficulties that might confront a "student soul" at each Plane, as well as its unique characteristics.

Because the Planes of Light are dimensions of vibration, you do not have to die to interact with them. The truths illuminated on the Planes of Light are present on earth—but you have to look inside yourself to find them. They exist not only spiritually but also biochemically. Each chakra, or energy center, of your body is located within an endocrine gland, and within each of these is a particular transitional metal, a nearly magical element that, when spun at the correct frequency, opens us to a corresponding Plane of Light and the healing it provides.

Dying activates this very specific transformation within the body, mind, and soul. But at that point, it's too late to bring the learning into your life. Why not, then, embrace the light—the lessons of the Planes of Light—while you are alive? If you do, not only will you not die when you die, but you will also be fully alive while you live.

So that you can begin this process of illumination during your lifetime, I have included discussions about how to dwell on the Planes right now. These techniques are not tricks. They are easy and manageable ways to live the full self—to live purposefully and joyfully without awaiting the illumination of the afterlife.

In my studies and reflections, I am constantly tugged toward yet another Plane. I call it the Thirteenth Plane of Light, although it is more a state than a place. Perhaps this is the "heaven" we are all seeking. When we are fully conscious, we become the self that we really are. We wake up and become fully aware. The soul that works its way through the Planes of Light naturally evolves into this state. We only need the willingness to be the blessed self that we are. In the end, being conscious is what being alive—and dwelling in the afterlife—is all about.

Our discussions will inevitably include reference to *the All*—one of many inadequate terms. What word can possibly describe the God, Light, Christ, Buddha, Krishna, Shakti, Spirit, Mother, Source, Divine, Self that we seek—and are becoming? Because of the many faces of the Creator, I may use any of these terms, depending upon the meaning I am ascribing. Feel free to substitute the one that speaks to you.

And now it is time to begin our journey. We will start by introducing you to my greatest teacher.

PART I

THE ENERGY OF
DEATH AND DYING

Long ago, a Lakota medicine man offered this explanation of life to me:

> *There is birth and there is death. In between is a corridor connecting the two. The key to living a good life is recognizing that there are no doors, no confines, no origin or destination. There is only the journey. There is no good or bad, only the integrity of how you do the walk.*

In Part I we will explore the journey into death, the end of the corridor. What really happens when we are dying? What happens after death? Other books have probed these mysteries, but this is the first to provide a step-by-step analysis of the energetic processes involved in the shift from life to death. It also offers the keys to incorporating the wisdom of death into our everyday lives and accessing the great White Light that many see at death to stimulate higher consciousness, healing, and well-being.

As you move through these chapters, know that you are really traveling the story of your own life, and lifetimes and death times—the story of your own evolution and transformation. While we all share the same process, our individual destinies are what we make of them.

CHAPTER 1

DEATH AS THE RIVER OF DREAMS

For life and death are one,
even as the river and the sea are one.

KAHLIL GIBRAN

n the introduction, I touched on my childhood attempts to learn all I could about death. My desire to grasp death's meaning only intensified as I grew older. For years, I searched for access to unseen realms. I wanted to penetrate the "other side," the worlds I intuitively knew existed. I wanted to understand what happens to the spirit, to the soul, when the body falls away. I was certain that if I possessed this knowledge, I could conquer my fear of death. And I suspected that my life would be enriched and forever changed.

My adult quest began in the jungles of Peru, and I could not write a book about death without introducing my most important teacher: the Vine of Death. This is a plant that for centuries has been used by South American medicine workers for healing, and to gain insight. When prepared correctly, it induces a trancelike state and experiences of other worlds.

I undertook several long voyages to learn from the Vine of Death. I would stuff a backpack and travel from Minneapolis to Miami, Miami to Lima, and finally from Lima to Iquitos. Once there, I stayed in a small hotel with a thatched roof, the walls open at the top. Sometimes the plumbing worked. The morning after I arrived, I would hire a boat and trek down the Amazon. On those occasions when the motor ran, the journey took a few hours, and I would relax and enjoy the monkeys on the shore, the birds soaring, the exotic, abundant life around me. When the motor did not run, the odyssey stretched much longer, across time and space, and while my guide labored with his oars or his pole, I entered a mind fugue of dreams.

Our landing was a village, just a few huts built around a store. When the store was open, we could buy canned goods, live chickens, cigarettes, maybe Coca-Cola. When it was closed, we had to walk door to door until we found someone to open the shop. I usually bought a few items and paid a dollar a bag for a steward, a young boy willing to carry backpacks for the equivalent of a week's worth of wages. He jogged while I trudged the six miles to Yushin-taita, the home of a shaman.

There, I learned. My instructors were the shaman, my own soul, and the spirit of the plant known to Peruvians as *Pachamama*. She was brewed into a vile-tasting concoction that, when imbibed, shocks the body into a deathlike state, thereby freeing the soul to "journey" to other realities—including those we find after death.

On my first trip, I had no idea what to expect. It didn't matter; I wasn't in charge.

During that first ceremony, I was flung out of my physical body. I looked down at myself, surprised to see that "I" was still sitting on a bench under a thatched roof, circled by twenty other people dressed in the white clothes of spiritual ceremony. When I looked up again, I found a beautiful African-looking female spirit gazing at me intently.

Her muscular arms were tattooed with blue serpents, which writhed as though alive. Her bald head seemed to reflect both the sun and the moon, and her feet were like tree roots, burrowing into the ground. She introduced herself as the Vine of Death, as the Pachamama.

She then presented me with a strange vision of a passageway, a portal in the universe. Suddenly, she was floating in the middle of this portal. On one side of her were the black of night and the stars of space; on her other side the light of day and creatures of nature. With one massive arm, she deftly swept up a star and deposited it in my forehead. With her other arm, she plucked a dark ball from my abdomen and threw it into the blackness. I knew intuitively that she was gathering the energy of death and bringing it into my living body, and with the same ease, lifting something of my life and bringing it to death.

I didn't get any further in my thinking, for I then became violently ill. But the next day I felt more vibrant than I had ever felt, and the psychic vision I had possessed since I was a young girl became even more focused. Pachamama had exchanged the energies of life and death—and I was changed.

Over the years I drank the Vine of Death eighteen times, gaining further insight with each ceremony. With her guidance, I was able to explore the hidden realms I had sought. Pachamama used vision, verbal instruction, and dreams to teach and then reinforce her central point: to live fully is to stand in the passageway between life and death.

Pachamama had shown me that information and healing can move between the living and the dead. But I wanted to understand how, so I began to actively seek answers in the world around me. I buried myself in esoteric material, indulging an ever-growing fascination with the chakras, the energy centers that I now believe transform energies from life to death and back again. I devoured books on quantum physics, instinctively drawn to a discipline that insists that "reality" isn't very real. I analyzed research on chemicals and metals that, it appeared, could make the visible turn invisible.

I gathered all the clues, but I knew that I was missing a piece. It fell into place on the airplane trip I mentioned in the introduction, during which I intuited the Planes of Light, the means by which wisdom is carried from death to life, and back again. After gaining insight into this energetic system, I was truly able to understand what Pachamama had worked to teach me: we are all capable of living a life that is much more real than we've ever dreamed of living. From her I learned to ask the question: why not live a life that measures up to our dreams? It is possible, but only if we embrace the wisdom of death and bring it into our living world.

I still journey to the Amazon, but I do not use the Vine of Death anymore, for I have learned that there is a universe within my own body. I can journey anywhere—and "anywhen"—on my own. And I now know that the ultimate odyssey will occur when my body falls away and death takes me deeper into my-self—and reality. As I had been sure would happen if I could gain this knowledge, I learned to stop fearing death: I discovered that death is a matrix of consciousness that links concrete reality with intangible reality.

During the ceremony of the Vine of Death, I was connected. The mosquitoes that swarmed around me brought messages from the ancients; the stars entered my body through the dirt beneath my feet. Over time, I have learned that I can attain this same level of interconnectedness in my daily life. My answers might be found in the witty remarks of my children. The stars might sing to me through songs on the radio. Tap water can be as alive to me as the water of the Amazon—and as the ultimate river, the river of death and life.

The Vine of Death introduced me to this river, but she didn't invent it. I splash in life—and death—all the time. The result-ing interconnectivity affords me the freedom to be adventurous, to open to invisible guidance, and to "reach for the stars"—my dreams—without fear of falling. If life and death are the same, what is there to be afraid of?

The instruction I received from the Vine of Death mirrors that of all great teachers and religions. Buddha, Christ, Mary, Black Elk, Ganesh, Krishna, Shakti, the Divine Mother: they all prepare us for death. While we are alive they gently (or sometimes forcefully) attempt to clear our dead thoughts, unhealthy perceptions, and spiritual lies. They show us what is important. They strive to bring that which is truly dead — our earthbound selves — to life. They ferry us along the river of truth to the reality we have known but do not remember.

You do not have to imbibe the Vine of Death to experience death. You do not have to go to a certain church, conduct a ceremony, or be a perfect human being to shatter the illusions of this earthly life. You only have to be willing to connect to death. This can seem frightening, but the fear itself can be illuminating, for it shows us where we need to "turn on the light" of truth and see clearly.

Why Explore Death? (And Why It Frightens Us)

We are collectively and individually fearful of death. We do not know what happens after our last breath or our last heartbeat. We do not comprehend what it means to live without a body. We wonder: Are there really ghosts, or guides, or angels, or spirits, or returning souls? Are the stories told by people who have had near-death experiences true?

Fools Crow was a renowned Lakota healer who helped thousands during his walk on this earth. He professed that death is a good thing. He said that after death, we journey with *Wakan-Tanka*, the equivalent of God or the Absolute. "In fact, this is what we are born for . . . born to die, for death is really the beginning of the great life He has in store for us."[1]

While most of us think that life holds our dreams and the potential to meet them, many spiritual leaders, deep thinkers, mystics, saints, and reformed sinners insist that death is sweet and that we do not need to be frightened of it. While we can easily acknowledge that without life there is no death, consider that without death there is no life. Nature teaches this. The dead leaves fall in the autumn to rot and fertilize the tree that produces new leaves in the spring. Think of death and life as dance partners. Think of life and death as currents in the river—different characteristics, yes, but flowing in the same direction.

Fear of death has its roots in fear of the unknown (or at least, the unremembered). Even if life is full of awful experiences, we have become used to them. We make decisions to protect us from pain, thinking that they actually make a difference. One of the most common is to close our hearts, so they can't be broken (again). Our attempts at control don't work, but they make us think that life is tame and that death, its seeming opposite, is wild. We are so busy trying to restrain life—to steer the river the way we think it "should" go—that we hardly ever get around to discovering our true dreams, much less pursuing them.

Life, however, is no more manageable than is death. It is even less logical than death. It sneaks up and surprises us, shifting our boundaries, or the parameters of everyday existence. Still, we are not as frightened of life as we are of death, because we have collectively agreed to ignore the fact that nothing stays the same. We rely on trite phrases like "history repeats" to run our lives, never bothering to notice that these sayings are lies. Each of us changes every moment of every day and every night. We never meet the world with the same self. How, then, can the past repeat itself? Life is as untamed as death!

We do not experience the newness of every moment—and the opportunity for new life in every moment—unless we face death. Dying before death tears the fabric of our reality. It opens us to the dreams we have locked away. By standing in the riptide between life and death, we can, if we want, begin to direct our lives by our dreams—by the stars within, not the rules laid upon us from without.

Life and death are continuations of the same spectrum of ideas. Together, they form the river of dreams. The only control we have is to dream of what we want and recognize ourselves in the dream around us. Through this recognition, we achieve a higher state of consciousness, which is our soul's main goal. By breaking free of the confines of life (and death), we can live the lives we desire. By embracing death right now, we can actually change our lives—and the world. As Dr. Paul Brunton, one of the pioneers in integrating Eastern and Western thinking, said, the "world is a dream grown to maturity."[2] Let us make sure that we are creating a self who is responsible enough to establish a mature world.

The Soul and the Planes of Light

To have passed into the afterlife is to be freed from the physical constraints of this world, but death does not eliminate what this world has taught us. Nor does life erase what we learn when we have passed. *Earth teaches us a way to be; death teaches us other ways to see.*

We come into this world from "somewhere else." And we leave this earth to go "somewhere else." Death is merely an entry point into other places of existence, some of which are quite similar to earth.

The difference between the realms of life on earth and those available after death is a difference of energetic frequency. The earth operates on a restricted spectrum of frequency or vibration; death provides access to other levels of existence. There are realms that move slower, deeper, and darker than the earth does. There is also a set of "worlds" that operate on a higher, quicker frequency and with more luminescence than does the earth. I call these the *Planes of Light,* for this is how they appear, both intuitively and scientifically. The Planes are ever-graduating levels of light that evolve the soul into higher and higher states of awareness and consciousness.

Why does the soul require evolution? The soul is a slowed-down version of the spirit or essence, the original self. Your spirit knows that it is eternally connected to the Greater Spirit and is continually bathed in love. Your spirit cannot be damaged; it can only become more illuminated and brighter. Life—the good and the bad of it—can only enhance, not detract from, your spirit.

This is not true of your soul, which is denser than your spirit. Your soul reflects the beauty of life, but also its wounds. There is a lot about life that causes harm, and to protect itself from injury your soul fills, or covers, itself with darkness. The dilemma is that this darkness causes the soul to forget its own light. And in forgetting its light, the soul stops living in the light. As a result, most souls "devolve" through life, rather than "evolve."

The solution is death, which opens the soul into planes of awareness that invite full remembering of the essential self. Death is a process, however, that starts long before we die—and continues through our physical death and beyond.

Consider This: The Story of Your Death

Suppose that you are a few years from death. You are not conscious of this fact, but your soul is. The part of your soul that has incarnated here to evolve, learn, and grow knows that its time on earth, in this body, is coming to a close; and it begins a slow and gentle process of readiness. As Plato suggested, life is a preparation for death. You are getting ready to seek Charon, the figure from Greek mythology who ferries the souls of the dead across the River Styx to the land beyond.

Unless you leave through a sudden death, there will be few noticeable changes in your body or demeanor. Yet the trained eye notices slight alterations. Your energy begins to concentrate into your heart, encouraging you to take more notice of relationships and your role in them. You become less devoted to things that were important to you earlier in your life. You become more involved in eternal questions, in your purpose. And you wonder about life after death.

The changes grow more profound as you approach death. The transformations begin to reach into your *energy system*, the complex set of energy organs that connect the body with the soul, and both with your spirit. Energies blend and separate, much as different streams in a river, until you lie near death.

At this point, changes are more perceptible, physically, energetically, and spiritually. Your physical stamina slips and your mind flutters from the past to the future, from the living to the dead. Your *chakras* and *auric fields*—energy bodies vital to your transition—alter substantially. If someone wore psychic eyeglasses, she would see you shift in color and energy, brightening into the brilliant light

26

that you have always been. Your soul quickens, wanting to awaken elsewhere. Spiritual beings, messengers of the beyond, begin to appear, participating in what is now an initiation process. Now several abrupt transformations begin to forge a doorway—and your soul, already loosened, separates from the earth plane.

And you awaken, out of your body, ready for another world.

Death: Journey into the Essential Self

What happens next is a journey into and toward your essential self. Vibratory tunnels appear, each leading to different dimensions and possibilities. The decision you make now affects your soul's next set of lessons and experiences.

Which "heaven" will you enter?

This is a more complicated question than you might think. The afterlife doesn't subdivide into paradise, hell, purgatory, or any other holding areas presented by most religions. *"Heaven" is a set of experiences, rather than a place.* It comprises levels of awareness: the Planes of Light.

These Planes are integrally connected to earth as well as the afterlife. I call them the Planes of *Light* because, as we shall explore in this book, we are all made of light, as is this world and the worlds after (and before) it. After death, a soul naturally assumes the next level of its progression, depending on the growth it has made while in a physical earthly body and its previous associations on the Planes of Light. Traveling through one Plane after another, a soul eventually graduates into the ultimate: the illumination of pure consciousness, the awareness of its divine identity.

Each of the twelve Planes of Light appears as a different level of development. Each is governed by its own set of masters, beings who excel at the lessons of a particular Plane and now teach other souls. Each Plane highlights certain vital truths necessary for transcendence. Moreover, each Plane has challenges that must be confronted.

These Planes are not only available after death; each can also be accessed while alive. While they stair-step "upward," as do grades in school, we might participate in a certain Plane and, instead of climbing to the next, return to "earth school" for our next set of lessons. We might transcend to one of the higher Planes and then suddenly need to return to a lower one, which holds the key to further advancement. The climax is the "Thirteenth Plane," which is not a Plane at all; it is a state of knowing. From here, we can go anywhere we want and do anything we need to do, including return to life on earth.

Why should we learn about these Planes while we're alive? Because life and death ultimately present us with the same goal: *to illuminate who we really are.* To illuminate is to provide light to make something visible. Life shines differently upon — or within — us than does death. In both places (or spaces), we discard previously unknown qualities, treasures, and attributes. Why not marry the twin beams of light and death, merging them into a spotlight that can showcase our true selves now? Our deepest wishes, our richest desires, can only be known or achieved through the evolution of our souls. Let us make the journey to the Planes of Light before death, and so be the light that we are while alive.

Perhaps we shall discover that this is the highest use of the Planes — the motivation for their "design." As we shall explore in the next chapter, we enter life from the realm of death. We are here on purpose. If we remember that purpose—if we awaken the knowledge of death within our living bodies—we will transform ourselves into the brightest of lights. We will illuminate the world.

THE PLANES OF LIGHT

The twelve Planes of Light are levels of awareness that invite soul evolution. To travel these while alive is to illuminate our essence—and to enhance our health, relationships, and work.

These are the major Planes, which culminate in a thirteenth "space" of consciousness:

1. *Plane of Rest.* A state of restfulness, where we are tended, assisted, loved, and taught how to receive.
2. *Plane of Evaluation.* Through a life review, we reexperience life from our own and others' perspectives, learning forgiveness.
3. *Plane of Healing.* Repair of soul wounds from the prior lifetime, often involving interaction with the living. The goal is self-responsibility.
4. *Plane of Knowledge.* Learning and assimilation of knowledge that relates to higher purposes.
5. *Plane of Wisdom.* Wisdom is experience tempered by knowledge—and knowledge enhanced by experience. Here, we integrate the two concepts and begin the true process of enlightenment.

6. *Plane of Truth.* What happens when we begin to actually embody spiritual truths, rather than simply reflect upon them? This is the basis of the Plane of Truth.

7. *Plane of Peace.* When we accept truth—opposites that merge into a unifying ideal—we achieve peace and integrity.

8. *Plane of Momentum.* Momentum is movement, the acceleration of spiritual purpose. It involves action toward a higher end—which is clarity.

9. *Plane of Love.* When we bring peace to others, we become instruments of love. On this Plane, we are invited to recognize that we are all made of love.

10. *Plane of Power.* Love in motion equates to power and the quest to recognize and open our spiritual or "charismatic" gifts.

11. *Plane of Charity.* Charity is the highest form of love. How do we "sacrifice" ourselves, while remaining whole?

12. *Plane of Mastery.* If we were to truly be ourselves, in every moment, what would we be masters "of," or more important, "for"? How does this relate to joy?

13. *The Illumination of Consciousness.* Technically, this is not a Plane. It's a state of awareness, which presents the eternal question: if I were made of love, what would I become—and do?

CHAPTER 2

THE FALL INTO DARKNESS: FROM DEATH TO LIFE

"How did you lose heaven?" Loki asked in a whisper . . . "Why did you fall into darkness?"

"Love." Merlin's wiry eyebrows lifted ruefully. "We loved Her. We loved Her more than anything. More than our lives. We would have followed Her anywhere. To hell itself." He snorted. "And we did."

"Who? . . ."

"God."

A. A. ATTANASIO

THE SERPENT AND THE GRAIL

We do not know exactly where we come "from." In fact, we have been told that this is not important. What matters, we are told, is where we are going after death, to heaven or to hell. Most of us are very aware of the mistakes we have made in this life; therefore, no matter what our priest, pastor, rabbi, or spiritual adviser might say, we do not really want to find out what is going to happen when we die. We are afraid of death. We think of life on earth as "safe," and death as "scary."

But the opposite might be truer. As the quote above reflects, earth is a fall into darkness. We have forgotten who—and what—we are. *We see only the shadows of our true selves.*

Nearly everyone who has a near-death experience reports being greeted by a great light. Little children often wonder why "the light turned off" after they came into this world. Perhaps it is when we are born that we truly surrender into darkness, and death returns us to the light that we are.

In this chapter we will examine the actual energetic structures of life and death. What is life really "made of"? How did we get here—and what "parts" of us are actually here? Why are we here? As we explore these and other topics, keep in mind that what we are really doing is telling your story—the story of your own soul, of your own life, death, and transformation. It is my hope that by the time you have read this narrative, you will know more about yourself, about your own destiny and brilliance. You will be able to identify why you are here and what you want to accomplish. By knowing more about yourself, you will be better able to understand others—and the world itself. By becoming more of the light that you are, you will help to light the world.

A Matter of the Spirit

Ultimately, we are all on this planet to achieve a spiritual purpose.

I cannot tell you what your purpose is, for it is unique to you. I can assure you, though, that it is vital, necessary, and enjoyable, and that you are here to influence others and the world in wild and wonderful ways. The ultimate carrier of your purpose is your most essential and primal self: your spirit.

Imagine that long ago you were a spark of light, happily illuminated within a big sun or greater source, one you might call the

Divine, God, Mother, Great Spirit, Krishna, Corn Maiden — any of the names assigned by various religious traditions. This is your *spirit*, or essence. It is your true self. At all times, it remains connected to the Greater Spirit, as if linked by a sunbeam.

What is the nature of this connection? In Genesis, we are told that God first created light. From a spiritual point of view, everything in and around you is made of light. At the quantum level, Dr. Richard Gerber, a pioneer in energy medicine and the author of *Vibrational Medicine,* states that the entire "physical universe is composed of orderly patterns of frozen light."[1] Gerber continues to assure us that, fundamentally, we are "spiritual beings of light which remain energetically connected to the Creator and the Creator's universe through a holographic connectivity relationship."[2]

You cannot injure a spirit any more than you can cut the air.

Everything animate has spirit and comes from spirit. As Gershon Winkler, an expert on Judaic shamanism, says, "Every person, every rock, every blade of grass, has a spirit that is spiraling it into existence and mirroring it in the spirit worlds."[3] Spirit cannot be destroyed, just as energy cannot be destroyed; it can only change form.

Death, then, is nothing to fear. Many cultures suggest that death is a release from the containment of life. In *The Sacred and the Profane,* historian Mircea Eliade compares the beliefs of the East Indian Ahrats with Buddhism. The Ahrats assert that at death we break open the "roof of our house," or the veil that keeps us from recognizing our sacred nature, and transcend the worldly experience. Buddhism teaches that we break the "cosmic egg," or "shell of ignorance," that we adopted at birth, and become the Buddha.[4] Both philosophies create a picture of release from darkness and flight into higher consciousness.

Death enables us to remember the light that we are.

Most spiritualists would nod at this statement and say, "Of course." But what does science say? Recent investigators are slowly following the trail of spiritual truth. Some of the most exciting findings reveal that we are, in fact, made of light and are interconnected through light. In her book *The Field*, Lynne McTaggart discloses research that substantiates both claims.

First, she shows that we are all interconnected in a field of light: research is revealing an energetic light field that connects everything and everyone, throughout time. Light is made of photons, which operate simultaneously as waves and particles. Similar studies show that the body itself is nothing but a biophoton machine, and that health is dependent on the flow of photons from the field to the self, and vice versa.[5]

I call this the "genesis field," and hypothesize that it is made of the very essence of the Source—the Great Spirit, the Creator—described in Genesis as the originator of all matter. If at some point there existed nothing but "the All," or God, and this God is known throughout the world as love, then what are the light, the world, and you made of but love itself?

The Bible says that we are made in God's image. The word used in this description is *Elohim*, a plural term for God that represents male and female, in unity. We are creator-beings, just as is God, only our spirits must journey out of the womb to *become* creator-beings.

Each of our spirits carries a certain set of spiritual truths. This is a lesson that I learned in a deeply personal way, and one that is continually reinforced in my work.

Throughout my twenties, I read scriptures from a variety of cultures that suggested this idea, but it wasn't until my early thirties that I had an experience that enabled me to fully understand it. I had a vivid dream, which came to me in the form of a memory. I recalled existing within a sphere of light — and not just any light. This light was alive, warm, and pulsating. I couldn't "see" the sphere in the physical sense, yet I was aware of everything that was going on within it; and I was surrounded by countless other beings. We were each unique, yet connected, safe in our differences — safe because there were no boundaries. My sense was of being in a deep sea, a womb, a place of beginning.

I was aching to get out, to leave the sphere of light. I felt like something — or someone — had just woken me, and it was time to move. A voice spoke from around me; it also seemed to emanate from within me. "You cannot leave without your task." A task? I felt simultaneously honored and terrified. "A special task," the voice affirmed. Now I was really scared — would I live up to expectations?

Suddenly, I was ushered forward by beings with wings of light and placed before three arcs of different colors. Then the beings guided me through each archway.

The energy of the first arc was multicolored and made me tingle. I heard the equivalent of the word "happiness." The second arc shimmered with sparkling shades of pink. I heard the word "healing." The third arc was deep and dark. Perhaps red? Maybe blue?

Or purple, the blend of both? A pleasant melody wafted from it, and I heard the phrase "sharing of love."

It was an initiation, and it transformed me. And I knew that the Creator had transmitted three essential energies — or truths — into my very being. It was my job to understand, reflect, and gradually become these three qualities, over time.

Since that experience, hundreds of clients have nodded at my suggestion that they carry certain spiritual truths, and that it is their mission to wield them effectively in all that they do. When I'm teaching, people relate their own stories. One older gentleman told me that an angel visited him when he was a child and gave him a "book of joy," instructing him about how to read it and share from its passages as he moved through life. A teenager tearfully shared that she used to tell her parents she was here to help "heal the earth"; sadly, they didn't listen to her. A young boy said that he had the same purpose, but with a specific duty: to "take care of the animals."

If the subject of purpose comes up when I'm working with clients individually, we usually slip into a regression — a return to that moment when the spirit separates from "the All," or the soul identifies itself with a purpose. I've conducted hundreds, maybe thousands, of regressions, and each individual quickly and assuredly recounts a spiritual truth or truths underlying his or her reason for acquiring a body and venturing forth from the All. These truths represent higher ideals, such as love, clarity, hope, or faith.

If seen from an earthly point of view, these truths would be perceived as tonal harmonics, or a series of colors and shapes. They constitute the basis of each individual's *spiritual purpose.* Your spiritual mission is to manifest your own unique version of these truths into concrete reality.

Thus, we are each here to sing our song, and together, to create a larger composition of beauty and delight. Truly, we are stars — beings of light — here to shine the heavens on earth, and transform the earth into heaven, a world made of love.

The Soul of the Matter

None of us would question that this world is disharmonious. The spiritual home, our original heaven, is composed only of unconditional love. But here is the irony: You cannot learn about unconditional love while in a state of unconditional love. To learn about unconditional love, you must experience conditions.

The spirit, in its perfection, is not an appropriate vessel for the journey into the unknown. It needs a vehicle to contain its immortal essence but gain experience and knowledge. It requires a soul.

Your *soul* is a slowed-down version of your essence. Whereas your spirit cannot be injured, your soul can. Whereas your spirit does not require instruction, your soul does. Your spirit knows that it is loved, but your soul has a choice. Your spirit cannot misunderstand the Divine or its own divinity; your soul can. *Through the soul, the spirit can dream its particular dream into three-dimensional reality, transforming the mere thought of a flower into a fragrant, blood-red blossom.*

There are many other terms for the word *soul,* among them *double, pneuma, shadow, psyche,* and *breath.* If you could read the story of your soul, you would know why you are what you are.

Your soul goes from lifetime to lifetime, not only learning during them, but also pausing for learning in between lives. These learning experiences allow your soul to manifest its spiritual purpose and to heal its soul wounds. This process of rebirthing is called *reincarnation.*

Your soul has become wounded through lifetimes of experiences. It has forgotten its essential goodness and believes itself separate from the All. Somehow, it must relearn what it is. How can the soul reconnect to its true self? This is the path of *soul evolution.*

The need to *evolve* is a result of a downward spiral of *devolution.* The Hopis believe that we have fallen far from the First World, *Tokpela,* or endless space, in which Spider Woman gathered the four colors—yellow, red, white, and black—mixed them with her saliva, and created men and women. We are now in the Fourth World, having declined in spiritual wisdom since the beginning.

Michael Cremo, an expert on the Vedic traditions, an ancient East Indian religion and philosophy, also asserts that we have gone downhill. He explains, "We did not evolve up from matter; rather, we have devolved, or come down, from the level of pure spiritual consciousness."[6]

Dr. Richard Gerber echoes these theories by stating that our "earth personalities forget that they are manifestations of the one supreme intelligence."[7] We must not forget, however, that we are able to return to full consciousness—that in fact, it is the "journey of spirit through the worlds of matter that provides the strongest driving force for the evolutionary process."[8]

If our essence is light, love, and goodness, how is it that we separated from these truths? *We followed "Her," or God, here.* We live in the dream of our souls. To create heaven on earth, we first need to understand the opposite choice, hell. To heal hell, we must heal our souls. That is the task of life—and of death.

The Flight of the Soul

Like your spirit, your soul carries the torch of your spiritual purpose. But it also holds your dysfunctional issues, all of which emanate from negative and inaccurate beliefs. To heal your soul—and your life and the world—it is important to understand the structure and flight of your soul. There is more to your story than that of spirit and soul.

After entering the material world, your soul acquired correct and incorrect learning based on experience. I first became aware of this truth when studying with a shaman in Peru. There was a small group of us, and no matter what life issue we professed to want cured, he would say, "Ah, negativity in the soul." Financial problems? A physical disorder? Depression? "Negativity in the soul." Since then, I have resolutely searched for soul-based rather than just physical-based causes for my own and others' problems. Inevitably, the issue becomes clearer and often resolves after the soul tells its story—a story that always speaks to an experience that has been misinterpreted.

Soul experiences can support spiritual experiences, of course. However, the harmful ones increase in number and intensity over time. Your soul, unable to hold onto the variety of perceptions forming its growing negativity, needed a mental storage vehicle. It created mind.

Your *mind* is the aspect of self that holds your soul's beliefs, which form the basis of your decisions. There are two main beliefs: correct and incorrect. The correct belief is *I am love.* The incorrect is *I am separate.* It is very simple.

These two beliefs further divide into six major positive and negative beliefs, which are:

- I am lovable (or not lovable).
- I am powerful (or not powerful).
- I am worthy (or not worthy).
- I am deserving (or not deserving).
- I am good (or bad).
- I have value (or no value).

Think about your life. Nearly every situation reduces to either believing that you are about love, or that you are separate from love. Almost every conflict in your heart and life comes from thinking you are unlovable, disempowered, unworthy, undeserving, bad, or lacking in value. Throughout every lifetime you have been (unfortunately) proving the accuracy of these negative beliefs. *Beliefs create perception, and perception creates reality.* For instance, even if someone is not being contemptuous of you, your belief in being powerless (or some other negative belief) may cause you to perceive cruelty. If you respond in kind, he or she might really start to torment you!

Our souls carry these beliefs—accurate and inaccurate—from one lifetime to another. In Hindu terms, the positive beliefs are called *dharma;* they fuel your spiritual purpose. The negative ones are *karma;* they must be transformed in order to become encouraging. Dharma supports your full essence and evolution through the attraction of kindly, joy-enhancing events. Karma also assists soul development, through the attraction of challenging experiences.

All soul beliefs, positive or negative, are encoded directly into your body at birth via the mind. Your *body* is the part of the self that impacts concrete reality. When embodied, your soul's beliefs are interpreted as what we can think of as *programs,* or specific ideas that operate your brain and central nervous system. These programs are based on the dharmic and karmic ideas held in the mind. When you enact your soul's programs, you create *patterns,* or repetitive behaviors that substantiate these beliefs.

Our souls return for one lifetime after another in order to reexamine the karmic programs and enhance the dharmic ones. Thus, we enjoy a complex and beautiful relationship between soul, mind, and body, which involves the transference of ideas from our souls into our bodies.

Clients frequently come to me to do "past life therapy" or to search through the annals of other lifetimes for reasons for today's events and issues. While I do believe in reincarnation, there could be other causes for these memories. They might be actual, personal memories, or ancestral memories; cellular memories—we have cells from billions of other people who have walked this earth; psychological constructs; psychic "reads" of others' memories; energetic charges held in a certain spot (i.e., leftover energies held in a "haunted house"); or even parallel lives—a quick flash in and out of an alternate existence. Whatever the case, our spirit knows the difference and will create whatever we need for our soul's evolution.

While each of us is alive, this evolutionary process is intricately linked to our energy system. As we will explore, the *energy system* is a complex set of energy bodies or organs. Energy organs are similar to physical organs in that they process energy (information that moves), with one key difference: your energy organs are able to convert spiritual energy to physical energy, and vice versa.

The primary energy organs are called *chakras* and *auric fields.* These organs are key in the soul's evolutionary journey. Indeed, they are the formative connection between the field of life and the field of death. As they create their own matrix, or field, in and around our bodies, these energy fields and organs ensure a flow between the world of the living and the worlds of the passed; they assist both.

🍃

FROM BEYOND TO THE HERE AND NOW

By what mechanisms does the soul enter our lifetime on earth? I have drawn from neurological research, metaphysical ideas, and studies in consciousness to create the following model. The detailed process of transferring ideas and programming from soul to mind and body involves:

- Soul programming into the *subconscious,* which connects the reptilian brain and the *Lower Mind.* The Lower Mind regulates your survival issues and basic physiology. If your Lower Mind thinks the world is a scary place, it will become so. If the belief in security dominates, you will find the world a safe place and will attract prosperity.

- Subconscious programming into the *unconscious,* which links the mammalian brain and the *Middle Mind.* Your Middle Mind manufactures feelings, thoughts, and emotions, which in turn determine your everyday behaviors. Negative programs result in negative behaviors and emotional issues including depression or anxiety. Positive programs will draw positive people and situations to you.

- Unconscious programming into *consciousness,* which bonds the higher or learning brain and the *Higher Mind.* Dharmic programs, if believed, can override karmic patterns, setting off a chain reaction in the body that results in achievement of spiritual purpose and easy manifesting. If karmic beliefs rule, life will be challenging and difficult. You will constantly feel like you are not living the life you are meant to have.

- The conscious self or Higher Mind opening to the *supraconscious,* a part of your spirit that interrelates the soul and the world. Your supraconscious is connected to the spiritual realms, higher truths, and divine assistance. Once located in the supraconscious, karma is automatically transformed to dharma. The problems and pains of the past can now be interpreted as "perfect," in that they led to learning and growth. This is not a justification for abuse. It is a healing process, one that recognizes the innate wholeness of every being and invites this wholeness into every corner of life.

Linking the Matrix of Life and Death:
The Planes of Light

I have used the phrase *genesis field* to describe the matrix of light that surrounds us. This field does not exist only for the living; it also assists in the afterlife.

I first perceived this field when I was a child, seeing it psychically as a fine, glowing mesh that interconnected everything and everyone within a room. I thought of it as a "fishing net of Christmas lights." Many years later when I began working with clients, I also saw this net, but it expanded beyond the room and into the greater universe. The strands or fibers of the net glowed more brightly when linking people who had a strong relationship—and even when linking people to animals and objects. When the relationship was weaker, so was the light. The matrix was thicker around families, and I could see strands of it flowing between the chakras of family members or highlighting specific auric fields.

Then one day I was working with a client whose mother had just died. I felt a rush of air in the room and perceived the entrance of a spirit. The mother? To my great astonishment, the spirit was surrounded by the same shimmering net of energy that I saw in and around the living. Moreover, streams from the matrix flowed into the daughter.

Through me, the mother passed on information that I couldn't otherwise have known, providing descriptions of their earlier life together as well as advice about the daughter's current life.

Then I experienced the healing power of the matrix. A great beam of energy opened up through the mother's wispy figure and flowed through into the daughter, entering the daughter's third chakra. The daughter, who had inherited kidney disease from the mother's family, felt a great heat enter her upper back, the backside entry of the third chakra; she nearly passed out — and at the time I was concerned. Later, she told me that her doctor had pronounced her kidney "healed."

My client's sister, who had the same disease, came to me for a healing session a few weeks later. Though we worked on her kidney, the mother's spirit did not appear to me, nor did the energy of the light. And unfortunately, the sister did not receive the miraculous cure. It had now become clear to me that the matrix itself possessed healing powers.

Since the day the mother's spirit came to visit her daughter and my eyes were opened to this extraordinary phenomenon, I have perceived that some deceased souls, as well as some living people, seem to be better able to command or accept energy through the genesis field than others. The healing is much more precise if the energy enters through one of the Planes of Light, which appear like tunnels in the matrix.

When we are born, our souls connect with the lower vibrations of the genesis field to translate the soul's spiritual properties into physical reality. Unfortunately, our poor souls are stunted from negative beliefs, and they join a human matrix or field that is also problematic. Psychically, this matrix can be perceived as a field of gray, murky clouds.

It is nearly impossible for us to free ourselves from this shadow while we are alive. We cannot perceive the light of others, much less our own. Earth *is* a fall into darkness. But death frees us from the human matrix, allowing us to better observe the genesis field and connect with the higher truths carried by our spirit.

The genesis field is structured into independent yet interconnected Planes of Light. These interconnecting Planes add up to the overall field and the truth of love that it represents. When we are temporarily released from the human matrix through death, our souls are better able to perceive these Planes of Light, as well as their own light. This is why I call these levels of awareness — these brilliant layers of heaven — *the Planes of Light.*

While "dead," our souls are free to travel these interdimensional Planes. The Planes graduate in frequency and luminescence until the soul reachieves its pure consciousness through recognition of its own light. Fundamentally, the soul reunites with its own essence. But our spirits do not simply become what they were before; our life experiences invite our spirits to become *more* than they were.

We are not finished with earth when we die. The lower Planes in particular interface with earth and encourage a review of earthly experiences. At any particular time, a soul might choose to return to earth, where its knowledge of light becomes concrete and tangible. The Planes of Light are actually higher-learning fields, with earth offering apprenticeship and practice. How do we transfer information and learning from life to death, and back? The transfer of information and learning comes through the energy system.

Our energy organs serve as prisms that transform spiritual energy into physical energy and back again. When we are alive, these organs keep us connected to the heavens. After we pass on, they retain our connection to the earth. They also enable us to travel the

Planes of Light when we are alive, so we do not have to "die when we die"—or lose our link to heaven while we live.

If you could journey the Planes of Light when you are alive, death would not need to be a healing for life. Life itself could be a healing state.

CHAPTER 3

DEATH: THE POWER OF A THOUSAND ANGEL WINGS

There were those songs
My mother
Never got to sing.

ROGER COOPER

The only time that many of us view reality from a higher point of view is after death.

When we are alive, we are surrounded by a web of shadows, a mesh of confusion spun by the combined negative consciousness of humanity. It smothers our true selves. We try to see clearly, but this "reality" gets in the way. At death, we are released from this network and are able to perceive more clearly. Death does have its advantages, as Malidoma Somé, an African shaman, suggests in this story.

Somé's father, dead for fifteen years, appears in his dream. To Somé's surprise, his father speaks in a language that he had not known when he was alive. Somé asks him if he can now speak French. His father replies that of course he can . . . because he is dead![1]

What do we experience when we are dead? Is it possible to learn this when we are alive?

The Lesson of Speedy the Mealworm

We have all been touched by death. One of my more poignant experiences did not even involve a person. Strangely enough, it instead involved a mealworm — named Speedy. I relate this tale as something of a "reality check."

I am not sure if you have ever been acquainted with a mealworm. From a child's perspective, mealworms are fascinating, inch-long creatures that amuse easily. They love being dangled from fingers, ushered across tabletops (especially if dinner has already been served and the peas can double as boulders), and stuffed into pockets to surprise grandmothers. From a mother's perspective, mealworms constitute the most questionable of God's creations, just above angler worms and way below caterpillars. Their most objectionable trait, from a mother's perspective, of course, is that unlike regular worms or caterpillars, they never progress — they only regress. Keep a mealworm around and you do not end up with a fish dinner or a magnificent butterfly: mealworms turn into beetles.

My son Gabe, a second-grader, had recently finished a science project in school having to do with mealworms. We inherited two of them from the project to raise to maturation. One had already entered the pupal stage, so it was not much more than a lump — nothing much to worry about (*yet,* the anxious mother thought). Speedy, however, who had previously been named Dog, lived up to his newly bestowed name. I have never met a busier mealworm.

All was well until one fateful morning when Gabe decided that Speedy would love to drive a race car. Gabe toted out his gigantic, remote-controlled machine, set Speedy on top, and began to play. Unfortunately, Speedy was not wearing his seat belt. He fell through a slit in the roof into the pit below the front seat.

I tried, I really did. I spent at least a half hour doing everything I could to rescue Speedy. I undid every screw with a table knife, pulled off every wheel with my nail file, and eventually sawed off the rooftop with a steak knife. Gabe participated by trying to shake Speedy out of the car—an unfortunate choice, as it proved. By the time I pried off the roof, Speedy was not so speedy anymore.

When Speedy was finally pronounced "passed," Gabe cried for at least an hour. "He was such a good playmate," he sobbed.

"Can you forgive yourself, honey?" I asked at one point.

"I don't know, Mommy," he said. "It's hard."

I sent Gabe off to school, his face puffy and tear-streaked.

That evening, Gabe prepared a coffin using one of my vitamin jars. On it he wrote a eulogy with permanent magic marker so that Speedy could read it from heaven: *Here is Speedy. He was a good meelworm [sic].*

Having done the right thing, Gabe continued with his life. He would raise four new replacement mealworms, gladly donated to the cause by his teacher.

I thought we were done with Speedy, but the morning after Gabe laid him to rest I actually had a spiritual "visitation" from a mealworm. At first, I did not connect the tall, beautiful, and iridescent figure with a mealworm, even one spelled "meelworm." The being glowed at the foot of my bed and spoke in a resonant, self-assured voice. "Thank your son," it said.

I was a little groggy, having been awakened from a deep sleep. "Who are you?" I asked.

"He will know," the figure said.

I thought quickly. "What am I thanking my son for?" I asked.

"For learning with me. Death has taught us both how to keep our hearts open."

Then the apparition disappeared.

Had Speedy really been an advanced being, or was I being overly imaginative? I may never be certain, but I am sure of this: death holds all kinds of surprises for us, including freedom from the make-believe everyday world that we think is "real."

Blurred Lines, Blurred Realities

The distinction between life and death is blurry at best, if one considers the incredible variety of stories about what happens after death. Certain traditions promise a resurrection—for the saintly, at least. Other traditions suggest that only men are rewarded after death, but women can tag along if they are nice to the men. Still other cultures teach that when our bodies return to the soil, we are finished—although we will continue through nature. Other traditions insist that only humans have souls, so only humans can go to heaven. Most cultures believe in reincarnation or some version of repetitive lifetimes.

In India and Pakistan, Hindus have no doubt about human reincarnation, but they add the caveat that higher souls can also transmigrate to the bodies of animals, especially cows. Hence, they refuse to kill cows or eat their meat.

In England, just about everyone gossips about the ghosts who live in their houses, and often cater to the whims of these invisible dwellers.

In Catholicism, it is said that to pray to the saints is to receive their blessings; one memorizes an extensive catechism of spiritual helpers to call upon for everything from ridding the house of insects to attracting a mate.

In the Hebrew tradition, Elijah is said to have ascended without dying, thereby establishing the idea that certain prophets might still walk with us. Angels do this, too, often disguising themselves in human form to test our spiritual merit.

The Chinese conduct rituals that revere the ancestors, whom they believe continue to guide them.

A particular tribe in Madagascar does not bury their dead for two years. Instead, they prop the bodies under trees and continue to receive their wisdom and help.

An herbal shaman in Belize provided me one of my favorite tales. "Plants might house the dead," he whispered, glancing around as if not wanting to be overheard. "Pick the wrong one, and they can drag you into their home."

Sure, I thought, inwardly rolling my eyes—until he shoved my face next to a flower. The petals wrinkled into a face that seemed to glare at me! I was sure that I was staring into a "possessed" flower, one inhabited by a spirit.

Such cultural stories as these—and those of your own culture—reveal an essential truth. There is no true separation between life and death. It is all a matter of perspective, and that perspective depends upon which side you are sitting on.

Death's Restorative Powers

We have all felt the sting of life's wounds. But whether we are still alive or have drawn our last breath, death has the power to heal whatever life has dealt us.

Much of our information about existence after death, as well as its healing powers, has been gathered from the stories of people who have died and returned to life; people who have had near-death experiences. NDEers, as they are called, are people who have been pronounced clinically dead and have then been restored to life, either miraculously or through medical means. Most are profoundly affected by the experience, spiritually and physically. Researchers studying them have compiled a body of evidence about death that points to the following:

- The continuous existence of the soul
- A series of steps through which the deceased passes after death
- A Higher Power that emanates love and grace
- Beings of love and light that provide guidance before, during, and after life's passage
- The possibility of several planes, dimensions, or types of existences following death

- The suggestion that at least some souls return to life
- The implication that what we do and believe during life influences where we go after death

If only a few people had reported these things, we would wonder about the validity of the conclusions. But according to a 1982 Gallup poll, approximately one person in twenty, or an estimated eight million adult Americans, has reported a near-death experience.[2] Another nationwide poll conducted in the 1990s raised the number to thirteen million adult Americans.[3]

These are the people who are reporting to us about death and illuminating the life thereafter. Some sources believe that there are even more people who are not talking, asserting that "slightly more than a third of those adults who come close to death today in our country undergo an NDE."[4]

Dannion Brinkley, a three-time NDE survivor, summarizes his experiences in this way:

- A sense of being dead
- Sensations of peace
- An out-of-body experience
- A tunnel experience
- Sighting of or greeting from "beings of the light"
- Greeting from a universal light
- A life review
- A reluctance to return to earth
- A personal transformation upon return[5]

All of these are common descriptions, echoed in the stories that Dr. Janis Amatuzio, a forensic pathologist, has heard. Dr. Amatuzio isn't a typical coroner. Besides performing autopsies, she has often talked to the families of the deceased. Her book, *Forever Ours,* is a collection of stories that have led her to believe that death isn't the end. Tales recounted include messages from the deceased and predeath visitations from already-passed loved ones.

Dr. Amatuzio also had an experience of her own. She was taking a nap one day and had an out-of-body experience; she was transported to a place of brilliant light, occupied by beings of light. They all knew her, and showed her how everyone is interconnected in a sea of bright sunlight. Amatuzio's conclusion about the experience was "that I was more than just my body. And that we are all deeply and profoundly connected—connected by love."[6]

People who return to life from an NDE are transformed. Most report a newfound or renewed belief in a supreme being, and faith in this being's goodness. They express a decreased fear of death—sometimes their fear disappears altogether—and a drive to live altruistically. They also report greatly increased psychic or healing abilities, all of which they use with a certainty of purpose. In fact, people who have had near-death experiences exhibit almost three times the number of verifiable psychic experiences as those who have never died and risen again.[7]

One of the most fascinating NDE stories I've heard involved a woman and her four-year-old son who both drowned when their car entered a flooded marsh. A voice spoke to the woman, telling her that it would be all right. Despite being submerged for half an hour, she revived.

Her son, however, was not so lucky; the child was pronounced brain dead. His organs had hemorrhaged, and if he were to live, the mother was told, it would be without consciousness. But the voice the mother had heard in the marsh instructed her again, telling her how to shift the boy's auric field and infuse him with positive energy.

For days, friends visited the little boy's body, now on life support. For twenty minutes at a time, they used what gifts they had to provide the child with loving energy: if the friend was a singer, she would sing; others would pray, or visualize the body mending. The boy has since completely recovered, and the voices of the "beings of light" insist that the same techniques can be used to restore the earth to her appropriate health.[8]

When we review reports of this kind, we see a recurring theme: *there is an implicit relationship between increased life powers and altruism and the acknowledgement of interconnection that we receive after dying.*

The Soul as Its Own Healer

How sad that when entering life the soul shuts its ears, eyes, and heart. How discouraging to believe that in order to enter the realm of time we must forget our own divinity. As a theosophical thinker from the 1950s put it, "We have made life a form of suspended animation . . . because it imprisons him [the soul] in time!"[9]

You could say that each soul creates each individual's problems. It carries forward karma and negative issues, and develops amnesia about dharma and lovability. As one of my mentors, a chiropractor named Dr. Michael Isaacson, used to say, however, the problem is the cure. Our soul is also the solution to our life's ills—because it can change. In his book *The Seat of the Soul,* Gary Zukav writes, "The individual unit of evolution is the soul," which can transform and grow because it is made of divine intelligence. In fact, a soul is actually God reduced to "individual forms, droplets, reducing its power to small particles of individual consciousness." If your soul would only realize its own selfhood and power, says Zukav, it would become larger and more Godlike—until it "becomes God."[10] While life is devolution from spirit, because of death, life can also evolve. It can know itself as the God that it is.

I have a client who experienced this power of her own God-self during a healing. She had metastasized breast cancer and was dying. Not knowing what else to do, I put my hands on her and began to pray. We both felt pulled out of our bodies and could see each other through our soul's eyes. As we talked about it later, we were shocked to find that we'd both had another experience—we were not alone! As my client put it, "There were at least a thousand angels, or at least their wings, wrapped around us."

That same day my client had a blood test. Her white cell count, which had fallen to nearly zero in tests the previous day, had risen to a normal level. She began to recover.

What really healed my client? Maybe previously received chemotherapy. Maybe the angels. Or maybe her increased, if temporary, perception—of the kind we do not normally acquire until we actually die. I do not know the answer. I do know, however, that we do not have to die to experience the gifts of death. Since the Divine has accompanied us to earth, the Divine has also provided a way for us to love on earth—and has constructed our bodies in such a way as to manifest this love.

To Die Before You Die

We are well equipped to live in beauty and grace. The experiences of individuals with near-death experiences dispel the notion that we have to leave this world to be free. Upon returning from death, people who have had such experiences live their lives differently. They emphasize sacredness, holiness, in their everyday lives.

Our physical bodies are already equipped to experience death before we die—at least, in terms of being able to experience love, light, and spirituality. Our brains are actually equipped for higher consciousness. Neurologists at the University of California, San Diego, have pinpointed a section of the temporal lobe that "appears to produce intense feelings of spiritual transcendence, combined with a sense of mystical presence."[11] Canadian neuroscientist Michael Persinger of Larentian University has reproduced such feelings in otherwise nonreligious people by stimulating this area. "One time we had a strobe light going," he wrote, "and this individual actually saw Christ in the strobe." Another individual experienced God visiting her. Examination of the electrocardiogram afterward reflected a classic spike and a slow-wave seizure over the temporal lobe during the time of the experience. Other parts of the brain were normal.[12]

Individuals who have meditated for many years often show these same brain patterns. Researchers including Dr. Margaret Patterson of Britain have found that applying electric currents to areas adjacent to the temporal lobe results in a high rate of cure for drug and alcohol abuse. Authors Melvin Morse and Paul Perry report that this effect mirrors the same transformative process experienced by people, alive or dead, who connect with the great White Light.[13]

We are equipped with the physical circuitry necessary to know death's lessons while we are alive. We are interconnected in a genesis field that links the living with the dead. But the real reason that we can transform death's gifts into life's gifts—and that we live after we die—is that we are energetic beings.

CHAPTER 4

THE ENERGY EXPLANATION: WHY LIFE AND DEATH ARE (ALMOST) THE SAME

Life itself is but the shadow of death.

SIR THOMAS BROWNE
THE GARDEN OF CYRUS, 1658

A few years ago a client called, wanting to discuss his just-deceased father. Hekko is Finnish and a descendent of Laplander shamans. According to his custom, the dead cannot rest until they impart their life learning to a loved one. Hekko wanted me to help him connect with his father.

This is the message that Hekko heard psychically: "It is not where you go, it is where you live, that counts."

The communiqué continued, with Hekko prompting for more. "I am that I am," his father said. "Even though you will not see, touch, or hear me again—I live, here, in your heart, as you do in mine."

Grieving people are often told that their deceased loved ones continue to live in their hearts. Most of us understand this message metaphorically; memories continue, as does our love. These things are true, but so is a literal interpretation of the statement. An energetic heart connection continues to exist beyond the boundary of life and death.

There is no real separation between what is concrete and what is not. There are no spaces between our dimension and any other. There is no permanent or real difference between the living and the dead.

In order to understand life after death—and more important, to gain the illumination of death while alive—we need a short physics lesson about energy. We'll start with the concept that everything is energy.

Everything Is Energy, in Death and in Life

When we are alive, we define ourselves by what we can see, hear, or touch. We are tissue, bone, and matter. When people die and we can no longer connect with them through our senses, we cannot help but think that they no longer exist. This is not true.

As Albert Einstein proved decades ago, everything is made of energy. Energy cannot be destroyed; it can only change form. You cannot *not* exist, you can only transform! Death cannot end your life, it can only enhance who and what you are.

Let's go back to our definition of energy: information that moves. Information is data that provides definition and instruction. Dr. Paul Pearsall, a medical doctor and expert on the relationship between love and energy, concurs that everything is energy. Since everything that exists is "full of information," energy is full of information.[1] Your hair stays on your head because cellular information tells it to do that. An airplane flies because information manages its functions. Toothpaste breaks down plaque because the chemicals within it effect this change.

But reality is not created by information alone. Do you think your teenager will clean his room just because you inform him that he should? Think again; better yet, talk. Intention makes information mean something.

We like to think that when we are alive we are safely anchored in the here and now. When we set our coffee cup on the table, we want to be able to pick it up again and resume our drink. Once divorced—of a thought, person, or feeling—we want to believe ourselves free. But the physical world is not that concrete.

I remember a client calling just after the terrorist attacks of September 11, 2001. He was a pastor who lived in a town near where the flight crashed in Pennsylvania. He reported that some members of his congregation, and he himself, had been experiencing inexplicable oddities since the tragedy. Many described silvery, ethereal figures walking through walls. One young girl saw an angel wrap its wings around one of the figures before both disappeared in a flash of light. Another woman set a peach pie to cool in a window. No one was around. She turned her back to open the refrigerator, turned again, and discovered that a slice had been neatly cut out of the pie. For his part, the pastor was having trouble with his morning coffee; he would pour a cup and it would slowly disappear before his eyes!

The victims of the flight were dead. They did not have bodies anymore; they had been burned in the crash. They weren't "there."

They could operate in and affect the third dimension, however, because on the quantum level, energy can be in two or more places simultaneously, and it can change form and affect other energies elsewhere. In fact, energy can exist as several forms at once! (For further information on the dimensions, see the sidebar in chapter 5.)

Science can explain this phenomenon. The reason that energy can operate so "creatively" is that all energy vibrates. Newtonian physics labels the continual dance of molecules as Brownian motion. If you look beneath the molecular level and into the subatomic or quantum scale, however, not only does everything vibrate, it vibrates in more than one locality! In fact, a particle might occupy two, three, or infinite spaces, time periods, or dimensions at the same moment—and move in every direction, all at once. It doesn't even have to remain a particle. It might transform into a wave one day, and then another day become both a wave and a particle simultaneously. As the NASA Office of Biological and Physical Research puts it, "Matter can be in two places at once. Objects can be particles and waves at the same time."[2] Actually, energy is not only *"allowed* to be in many places at the same time, it is in fact *required* to be there (and there, and there, and there)."[3]

The simplest bit of matter reveals this same propensity. You can't get any less complex than the neutron, which is neutrally charged. As MIT scientist and author Seth Lloyd reports, this supposedly simple particle doesn't vibrate in one direction alone. It spins "clockwise and counterclockwise at the same time." Quantum particles not only speak in the language of yes or no, they speak yes *and* no simultaneously.[4]

Another concept, called *entanglement,* expands the connection. If two particles have associated, they will affect each other, no matter where they are. Let's say that Particle Bob and Particle Betty were once . . . involved. During their relationship, both were positively charged. Bob gets mad and trudges off to Mars — obstinately flipping negative instead of positive. Guess what: as soon as Bob shifts, so does Betty!

We're not through yet, though. Now Bob meets Wendy Wave and falls for her head over heels. Happy once again, he turns positive. Without knowing why, Betty feels Bob's afterglow — and she shifts as well.

On the quantum level, we can be everywhere — and every "when" and "who" — at once. We're not going to perceive these alternative realities while we are alive, however, because of yet another simple scientific truth.

The Cat's Meow: Dead and Alive at the Same Time

Enter the tale of Cat, who belongs to Austrian physicist Erwin Schrödinger. Cat is unique in that he exists on the quantum plane, the land of disappearing and reappearing quanta. Cat is just like any typical cat, busy mousing and catnapping. But because we live in quantum land, we are going to play a trick on Cat. We are going to make him alive and dead at the same time.

Simultaneously, we will feed Cat poison and nutritious food. In quantum land, Cat is now dead — and alive. In the third dimension, however, we are only able to perceive one of these realities. This is because of a simple physics truth: an observer affects the outcome.

On earth, we have unconsciously agreed to certain "natural" laws. One of them is that if you feed a cat poison, he will die. If we override this law and apply a different one—perhaps, that poison is good for you—Cat will happily slurp his poison and live to see another day. We become what our environment tells us to become, and in turn, we keep creating a reality that seems "true." We associate reality with the "human matrix" we have invented, not even realizing that *we are writing the script for it as we go.*

When people die, they continue to be affected by their earthly loved ones. Christians associate death with heaven and hell. Guess what the deceased Christian soul will tend to experience? Christian NDEers overwhelmingly associate the afterlife with heaven, but there are also reports of hell. What about the numerous cultures that believe in ghosts, the supernatural, the effect of the ancestors, visitations of the dead, and the ability of the living to cross over into the realms of the afterlife? Are they wrong? No. They believe what they believe, and that becomes true. Perception creates third-dimensional reality—but it does not create all realities. For every reality we see "here," there are thousands of alternative—but just as real—realities elsewhere. Do we desire to see Cat alive or dead—or both? That is the question we must ask ourselves.

🍃

THE MYSTERY OF HELL

Like many of us, I have long puzzled over the belief in hell, not understanding how a God of love would punish us for all eternity. One night, I went to bed and had this dream about "hell."

I gazed into a fiery pit where people writhed in pain. Everyone looked similarly miserable, until I noticed that there were dazzling winged beings struggling alongside the "normal" individuals. I believed them to be angels. As I watched, I saw several angels carrying children out of the pit on a golden ladder. One of the angels was toting a particularly young child who was laughing and gurgling. The angel turned and looked at me, explaining the ease with which he and the other angels could rescue the children.

Through his story, I came to understand that hell is created from belief. People enter and remain anchored in this space, which is formed by thoughts, because they believe hell exists and that they are so "bad," it's all they deserve after death. Children, however, can't fabricate a hell—they can only adopt their parents' beliefs. Angels can therefore rescue children from hell because the belief holding them in place isn't very strong.

My lesson about hell continued. As I watched, I noticed that a woman trailed the duo, climbing the golden ladder in their wake. The angel explained that this woman was the child's mother. Her maternal love was so strong that it overrode her confidence in hell. Below them, however, a man continued to swim in the anguish, even as he watched the mother and child ascend. I had a sense that he was the child's father, the woman's husband. He shook his head, as if dismayed that they were breaking "God's law" by leaving hell.

My heart nearly shattered. Why didn't he leave with his family? What internal torment kept him stuck in this literal hellhole? Was he lost, eternally?

An angel prompted me to peer closer into the conflagration. Some of the inhabitants of hell were really angels in disguise. I had a sense that hell's victims couldn't distinguish the angels from their fellow inhabitants, and that this was the point. What better way to help the self-damned but to seem equally condemned? But even though a few of the camouflaged angels were encouraging the man to leave, he remained obstinately fixed in place. I asked why.

"He wants to prove the accuracy of his beliefs," the angel responded. "Having condemned others with his hatred when alive, he now condemns himself."

Many studies and theorists have revealed that perception follows belief. At death, one soul might perceive Christ, another Krishna. Our minds convert the inexplicable into images it can understand. At the same time, the combined consciousness of many—if not millions of—"objective observers" can form a field or environment that can actually "create" a reality. Consider the numerous visitations by Virgin Mary throughout Europe and the Middle East in the 1800s. According to philosopher Michael Grosse, these visions are most likely "hologramlike projections" created by the collective unconscious—not true interactions with the historical Mary.[5] Certainly, we can entertain "real" angels, saints, and prophets—but a strong notion like hell can also create the very hell we want to avoid. And would not a loving Creator do anything within its power to convince us of the unreality of hell—even when we think it's "too late"?

It's often easier to perceive expanded realities and choices after passing. I recall the story of an eighty-year-old man named

Gardner who took a class on psychic gifts that I was teaching at a church. He had clinically died during surgery and returned to life.

Gardner told the class that while dead he had been lifted from his body by two angels, who brought him to a garden where a beautiful woman greeted him. (At this point, Gardner looked over at his wife, a bit abashed, but she just smiled.) The woman smiled and then put her hand on his heart.

Gardner was awash in emotions, and cried for what seemed like an eternity before she lifted her hand away. Then the angels returned and plunged Gardner back into his body. He found himself suddenly back in the operating room and could see not only the people around him, but also his loved ones, who were sitting in a waiting room.

He didn't see his aged wife, or the worried eyes of the surgeon. Nor did he feel the anger toward his son he had harbored for many years, or concern he'd had about his daughter's husband. Gardner related to us that it was "as if I could only see through my heart" and "only see the good and the truth." When someone in the class asked him what the truth was, Gardner said, "that everyone is trying to be loved or loving, just not in a very good way."

After Gardner spoke, his wife added her assessment of the near-death experience. From her point of view, Gardner had been a hardened, negative individual before the event. He was now loving and soft—and psychic. Gardner affirmed her statement, saying that each night he now received dreams showing him people in trouble and how he could help them.

The class had sat raptly as he told his story, but now everyone began to talk. Yet another elderly woman, Jane, had died when having her fifth child. After drifting out of her body, Jane became aware of a tunnel above her head and a white light streaming into the room. Her sense was that the tunnel and the light had always been present, but she hadn't previously noticed them.

Jane wanted to leave. Her husband was abusive and she was tired of life. A nurse named Catherine, however, stepped forward to hold on to Jane's drifting form. Catherine told Jane about her fifth child, which would be a son, and the difference he would make in the world. Finally, Jane agreed to stay. She slipped back into her body and continued giving birth.

Jane's fifth child—a son—went on to start an international nonprofit to assist victims of war and natural disasters. Though she called the hospital later to thank the nurse, she was told that there was no nurse named Catherine on staff—nor had there ever been.

I hear these kinds of stories almost every day. Are the perceptivity and loving heart Gardner now has only available to people who have died? Are we always surrounded by angels—and white lights and tunnels—but, for some reason, just can't see them unless we die? What we call "otherworldly" surrounds us all the time, but everyday life usually keeps us from perceiving it. Death doesn't change reality; rather, at death our soul, freed from the amnesia acquired at birth, expands in consciousness. The human matrix falls away. Depending upon the soul's true character, level of development, and individual goals, it sees more and can therefore become more.

How does this happen? It's not complicated: the soul simply shifts in its ability to recognize and work with information and vibration. As we will explore in the following sidebar, there is a simple but little-known application of physics that explains the afterlife enlightenment process. Basically, the soul experiences a reversal of entropy.

WHAT ENTROPY HAS TO DO WITH IT: THE "DOWNHILL SLIDE"

In physics, there are two types of information. There is visible information—information we can access when we are in the state of matter—and there is invisible information, also called *entropy.* Entropy is a measure of the "bits of *unavailable* information" in the world, or in us.[6]

We have all experienced the "downhill slide" of entropy. Remember cramming for a school examination? Yes, at some point you knew what year the Americans dumped tea into the Atlantic or the date the British invaded the Falklands. If you happen to still remember these details, I bet there are millions of other bits of data you have lost over the course of your life. Natural law determines that, over time, everything in the universe loses ground, unless we are able to apply an ever-increasing amount of energy—which we cannot. Hence, we forget. We age. We die.

As Seth Lloyd explains, the "missing" information—or energy—does not actually go away, any more than Cat's living self disappears when he dies. Rather, the unused information or energy slips into a seemingly unavailable "dimension" or "parallel reality." If we return to our analogy from chapter 1, the river of death

71

and life, it is as if we proceed in life on an ever-narrowing channel—the "lost water" still flowing alongside us, but inaccessible.

How can we access what we think we've lost? Discover the truisms hidden within the matrix of human thought? We turn to the light.

CHAPTER 5

IT'S ALL
ABOUT LIGHT

*The existence of man is built on foundations
of iron laws and principles.
But the daily and prosperous life is built
upon the lightest touch.*

MOYSHEH OYVED
GEMS AND LIFE

One of my clients is a famous musician. He was not always famous, nor a musician, nor, by his own report, a good person. He was living the "fast life" of sex, drugs, and rock and roll when he experienced something that propelled him beyond this lifestyle.

"I saw the light," he reported, sheepishly adding, "I know, it sounds religious, but it was not." He shared that years earlier he had been sitting at his kitchen table, shooting cocaine, when the room became dark. Suddenly a light switched on in his brain, catapulting him into a never-before-experienced "sense of euphoria and 'rightness' with the world." He explained further: "It was not

73

a being; it was more than that. I knew that it was not mad at me for my lifestyle; it was concerned for my life."

My client went into drug treatment, after which he began hearing music in his head. These sounds have kept him at the top of the ratings charts ever since.

I cannot recount the number of times I have heard of similar life-changing experiences, from individuals who have had near-death experiences to children recalling what God is like. Most of these anecdotes share a common element: there is a light or an enlightening experience that changes their lives. There is a reason for this.

It all comes down to the light: the light beyond, the light within, and the light that we are.

From Light to Light . . .

The Genesis story of the Bible says that we are created from earth, and that when we die we return to earth. But we are not made of mud; we're made of light.

Everything consists of photons and the subatomic particles that compose these wave-particles. We have already discussed this fact, but I have not shown you exactly what this means in reference to death. The clearest way to explain life, death, and the illumination capabilities of the Planes of Light is to provide a verbal "diagram," also represented in the illustration on the next page.

Your spirit emerges from the Source, the great sun of eternal light. It can be thought of as a bubble of light, bounded by its own individual nature. Inserted into this bubble, your spirit, are twelve

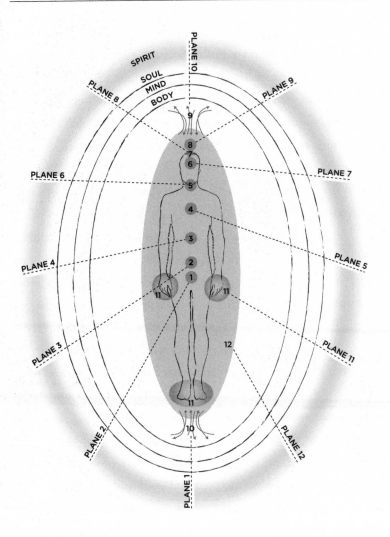

bands of light, sunbeams that emanate from the greater Source. These twelve bands, or Planes, when they are gathered on top of one another, appear as a rainbow. The higher, ultraviolet energies spin upward into colors so bright and light that we cannot see them with our physical eyes. These regulate spiritual matters. The lower, infrared beams are so dark and unfathomable that we cannot perceive them either. These direct the concrete and tangible. These are all the Planes of Light, independent levels of wisdom.

Why would your spirit require these somewhat limiting spectrums of knowledge? Boundaries are necessary to create a personal self—even spiritually. Also, divine love dictates the need for permanent connection and flow. The Planes of Light answer both conditions.

Step into the spirit bubble and you'll perceive a soul bubble. Within it, there is a mind bubble and within the mind, a body bubble. Inside the body are the chakras, each of which is based in a physical endocrine gland. The Planes of Light have the potential to penetrate each layer—but they usually don't, except for a necessary and permanent link with the chakras. More often, our own issues congest the connections, cutting us off from divine wisdom.

Each Plane interacts with a different dimension—a point that will become important as we examine the role of light in life and death. At death, the chakras and Planes interact to shift the "this-life" bodily knowledge into the mind, soul, and spirit. Light plays a critical function in this process. It can clear at least some of the blockages between aspects of self. At birth, the chakras and Planes interact to spin information from the greater aspects of self into the body. Again, our various blockages will determine how much we will acquire, access, or remember. During life, our ability to "open" light determines our health, happiness, and welfare. Bottom line: it's all about light.

THE TWELVE DIMENSIONS

Through my study of quantum and Newtonian physics, mathematics, and esoteric philosophy—particularly the Egyptian knowledge of the dimensions—I have determined that there are twelve dimensions, which occupy specific places in the space-time continuum:

First dimension: A point; the zero place of the beginning; space.

Second dimension: Lines; vertical and horizontal lines combined to form shapes with length and width.

Third dimension: A cube; structure. Height is added. Objects now exist, and you exist within the structure of the cube. If you cut the corners of the cube, you produce triangle shapes and a tetrahedron, the sign of balance and equilibrium. The tetrahedron is also the sign of divinity.

Fourth dimension: A point outside the cube. You are still in the cube but can access time outside of the box to shape the cube.

Fifth dimension: A cube with lines outside of it. You now exist within or outside of the cube, but not in both places at once.

Sixth dimension: The cube lines dissolve and leave only disconnected points. Each point becomes an opening for creation.

Seventh dimension: No points and no lines; accesses White Light.

Eighth dimension: Nothing and everything. This is the power of love and imagination.

Ninth dimension: Movement through stillness. Expressed love.

Tenth dimension: Time and timelessness. Expressed in cycles of the natural world.

Eleventh dimension: Purity with all.

Twelfth dimension: Unity with the Creator.

The Healing Power of Light

Modern science is amazed by the power of light. You experience its miracles every day without even thinking about it. Sunlight, for example, stimulates your pineal gland, inviting happiness, ease of mind, and the production of hormones necessary for sleep.

New research applying high-intensity light of varying colors is showing promising affects on everything from viruses to Alzheimer's disease. Apparently, light works on the cellular level in the body, transferring energy to the mitochondria—a part of the cell—which in turn helps the body to heal itself. Light also affects the speed of certain chemical processes.

The key to the therapeutic use of light is to choose the right color or wavelength. Infrared light has been shown to reduce the severity of a heart attack by up to 50 percent, reverse blindness in animals, and heal oral sores. Red light helps wounds heal more quickly and reverses skin aging. Blue light as well as red light can kill bacteria. Blue light can also reset the biological clock, treat seasonal affective disorder, and help people with Alzheimer's disease sleep better at night. Ultraviolet light keeps bacteria and viruses from reproducing, and can sterilize air and water.[1]

The most healing light, that which embraces souls at death, is the great White Light. This light stretches through all dimensions to connect us with the All—and may even *be* the All.

"Zero-Point Light": The White Light of Death

Most individuals who have a near-death experience see a great white light at death. Many describe this light as consciousness emanating unconditional love. There actually is such a light and it is, "on earth as it is in heaven," related to a phenomenon called *zero point.*

Studies are revealing that there is a zero-point energy field that resides in stillness and yet maintains continual motion. Scientists have long looked for explanations of what we would call the miraculous, and zero-point energy seems to be it.

The phenomenon begins with chilling something a few billionths of a degree above absolute zero, almost three hundred degrees below zero centigrade. Atomic motion stops—but energy continues. An experiment done by researchers including Lene Vestergaard Hau demonstrated that light was frozen to a standstill at "zero" velocity or speed, which means that light vanished. Its imprint, however, did not! The "disappeared" light regenerated when stimulated by yet another light.[2]

Only quantum theory can explain why the background radiation continued to emanate—why something can move even when completely still. The particles might not be moving directionally, *but they could flash in and out of existence.* The implications of this finding are staggering.

For example, skeptics ask why only some people remember past lives. According to researcher Walter Schempp, memory is not stored in the brain, but rather in what I call the *genesis field.* This field is composed of zero-point light.[3] Memories of the past, parallel existences, ancestral events, or even the future flash in and out of existence—or in this case, awareness—based on our relationship with the field. If our light is "on," we will remember. When the departing soul sees the light, memories flood in. The light from the Source frees the soul from its frozen state.

The fact that we are made of light—that the body itself is a biophoton organism—has been well established by several researchers, including Fritz-Albert Popp. One of Popp's findings was that DNA itself is a storehouse of light, or biophoton emissions.

The more photons that are emitted from an organism's DNA, the higher it stands on the evolutionary scale. The zero point or genesis field plays a central role in originating and responding to this internal light. If a body of photons internalizes too much or too little light from the field, disease results. Popp concluded that organisms are healthiest if they rely on a minimum of "free energy." This means that they each approach their own zero state, or nothingness.[4] Essentially, we can, and need to, generate our own light.

This explains how a soul can be integrated into the body one moment—and then be gone in the next moment. It is not destroyed; it merely blinks into another pocket of the universe. This shows how our spirits, with their infinite wisdom, can surround our bodies and why sometimes knowledge is available—and then, suddenly, is not available. This also reveals the true nature of the

White Light: a consciousness that operates at zero point produces a zero-point field, and always holds us, even when we do not recognize it.

This is the story of the spirit. When you enter the physical realm, your spirit "freezes," at least relative to your everyday consciousness. You cannot see, hear, or touch it, because you are identifying chiefly with the "imprint" that it leaves: your body, which is encoded by your soul and mind. At death, a light—the *White Light*—restimulates your spirit. The body disappears, not because it does not exist anymore but because the more ethereal parts of you, such as your soul, reabsorb the body's essential qualities or energetic charges.

The shift from body to soul is accomplished while we are dying and just after the body dies. The transformation from soul to spirit usually happens after death through the Planes of Light, which expose us to higher and higher frequencies of light. And there is yet another energy body that interconnects the physical body with the soul body. The Ancient Egyptians called it the *Ka*. The Ka is the "light body," and it is fed by light. Most often, the light body is not provided the light it needs to generate until we are dying, at which time the ill are often described as "glowing." You can, however, activate the light body, as well as your physical body, through the chakras while you are alive. It is simply a matter of knowing how.

The most vital entryways for light in the body are the chakras and the auric fields. These energy centers not only convert low-spectrum to high-spectrum light and back again, but also fast-moving energy to slow-moving energy and vice versa.

Prisms of Light: Your Chakras and Auric Fields

Your chakras are spinning organs of light that regulate your internal body. The word *chakra* comes from a Sanskrit word meaning "wheels of light." Chakras can process all frequencies of light or information energy. Therefore, they can convert psychic information to sensory data and back again.

Contemporary studies at major universities, including Duke University and the University of California, Los Angeles, are documenting the existence of chakras. Valerie Hunt of Stanford University, author of *The Science of Human Vibrations,* has produced striking documentation, and healer Rosalyn Bruyere describes applications of Hunt's work in her book *Wheels of Light.* Bruyere explains that chakras are not simply New Age or mystical phenomena but actual organs, the sounds and locations of which can be found within the body.[5]

Each chakra is paired with an auric band. These bands combine to form an overall auric field, also referred to as the aura, which consists of graduated layers of light that manage the energy outside of your body. These auric layers link to the chakras, creating a symbiotic relationship to manage events inside and outside of you. A partnered chakra and auric field also relates to a specific Plane of Light, one of the levels of awareness that ultimately link us to the Source.

The chart on the next page shows the location of each chakra and auric field, the color and quality associated with each, and the corresponding Plane of Light. You will notice that, while most auric layers emanate in order from the first outward, the exception

CHAKRA, LOCATION / FUNCTION	AURIC FIELD	COLOR	PLANE OF LIGHT
FIRST Groin / Safety and security	FIRST Skin and next to skin	Red	SECOND Plane of Evaluation
SECOND Abdomen / Feelings and creativity	SECOND Next to tenth field	Orange	THIRD Plane of Healing
THIRD Solar plexus / Mental clarity and power	THIRD Outside second field	Yellow	FOURTH Plane of Knowledge
FOURTH Heart / Love and relationships	FOURTH Outside third field	Green	FIFTH Plane of Wisdom
FIFTH Throat / Communication	FIFTH Outside fourth field	Blue	SIXTH Plane of Truth
SIXTH Forehead / Vision, futuring, and self-image	SIXTH Outside fifth field	Purple	SEVENTH Plane of Peace
SEVENTH Top of the head / Spirituality, prophecy, and purpose	SEVENTH Outside sixth field	White	EIGHTH Plane of Momentum
EIGHTH Just on top of the head / Karma, connection between worlds	EIGHTH Outside seventh field	Silver	NINTH Plane of Love
NINTH A foot and a half above the head / Soul bonds, harmony, unity	NINTH Outside eighth field	Gold	TENTH Plane of Power
TENTH Under the feet / Natural world and lineage	TENTH Outside first field	Brown	FIRST Plane of Rest
ELEVENTH Around the body, especially the hands and feet / Ability to command natural and supernatural forces	ELEVENTH Around the entire body, inside the twelfth field	Rose	ELEVENTH Plane of Charity
TWELFTH Around body, inserting into body through thirty-two secondary points / Personal mastery	TWELFTH Around the entire body, outside the eleventh field	Clear	TWELFTH Plane of Mastery

is the tenth, which serves as an etheric body right outside of the first auric field. Therefore, the Planes of Light are out of numerical order, in that the initial Plane actually correlates to the tenth chakra and auric field.

Each chakra also regulates a specific endocrine gland, which is affected by an alchemical substance that responds to the zero-point or great White Light. And buried within these glands we find the topic of the next chapter—the true magic of light, which I call *metals of light.*

CHAPTER 6

GETTING TO ZERO POINT: METALS OF LIGHT

magine that you have joined an archaeological expedition, one conducted decades ago in a dark and ancient temple in the Sinai desert. You are an assistant to Sir W. M. Flinders Petrie. Neither of you knows it, but you are about to discover how humans can become the illuminated beings of light that they really are.

With Petrie, you and the team have unearthed a temple dating back to 2600 BC. Your key discoveries include the Egyptian artifacts you expected to find—but there is something else. You have found a mysterious cache of pure white powder (tons of it, in fact) and a metallurgist's crucible.

You have discovered the powder of light, an earthly rendition of the White Light that is met after death.

We have established that each chakra and auric field is associated with a different Plane of Light. We might picture the chakras at the center of a circle called "the body." The sphere of "the mind" surrounds the body, "the soul" encircles the mind, and "the spirit" encompasses them all. The Planes of Light are beams of wisdom—levels of learning—that link with and feed the spirit during our lives. But our own blockages and problems keep them from penetrating to our core.

Each chakra is also connected to an endocrine gland. This fact becomes vitally important to those of us who long to activate the wisdom of the Planes before we die; the physical nature of the chakras lends itself to physical transformation. Each endocrine gland possesses yet another physical property which, when enabled, leads to the ultimate metamorphosis—becoming our own spiritual self while we live.

This awakening is possible because each gland (and chakra) contains a transitional metal—a magical, alchemical, and very concrete element—that, when spun to zero point, allows a chakra to transform its corresponding Plane of Light into concrete matter. This incoming light, in turn, fills the chakra with the wisdom of the associated Plane and performs tangible, physical healing.

My research into this process has astounded me, leading me to a full realization of the wonder of the world. This quote captures my astonishment:

There are more things in heaven and earth, Horatio,
Than are dreamt of in your philosophy.[1]

The Magic Matter of Transitional Metals

The explorer you joined in Egypt at the beginning of this chapter was a real man who found a magic powder of antiquity. But what was it? And what did it have to do with the transformations that occur after death—and that are possible during life? Many now link this powder with an Egyptian substance called *mfkzt.* When used correctly, it was said to awaken the light body, or Ka, of the ancient Egyptians, helping them achieve the *Plane of Shar-On,* or the Dimension of the Orbit of Light. As Laurence Gardner explains in his book *Lost Secrets of the Sacred Ark,* reaching this plane was equivalent to gaining enlightened consciousness, and to the Egyptians was a way of releasing the soul, so it might achieve immortality. Gardner weaves a drama of light, alchemy, life, and death, and coins the term the *Field of Mfkzt,* which I call the genesis field.[2]

Gardner makes a case that this powder is also what is referred to as the Philosopher's Stone, the Ark of the Covenant, the Holy Grail, and *manna* from the Bible. It is a result of using transitional metals to achieve the higher planes of awareness. Before we shake off his claims as New Age nonsense, let us look at scientific probes into the function of this powder. It really does exist as a range of elements that generate light for healing and awareness—a group of metals called *transitional metals.*

The Magic of Transitional Metals

Transitional metals are elements with uncertain and changeable electron charges, either positive or negative. All atoms have valences, or orbits, that carry their electrons. The atoms in typical metals are usually positive or negative: full or empty. Transitional metals are not really either—they are always half-full or half-empty. Most atoms cluster in groups of at least two or more. A transitional atom, however, can be created within or remain within a stable, single atomic state called the *monatomic state*. Because of this, transitional metals are also referred to as *monatomic metals.*

Back in ancient Egypt, the best known and most widely used monatomic metals were gold and members of the platinum group. These include iridium, palladium, rhodium, osmium, and ruthenium, as well as platinum. The current list of transition group elements occupies the middle thirty-eight elements of the periodic table. These elements are the focus of thousands of government and corporate studies, for they can produce seemingly miraculous results. A summary of a few of these studies reveals the following effects of certain transitional metals:[3]

- Iridium and rhodium have antiaging properties.
- Ruthenium and platinum compounds interact with DNA.
- Gold and platinum can activate the endocrinal system to heighten awareness and aptitude.
- High-spin powdered gold affects the pineal gland, increasing melatonin production. This unique element begins as yellow gold that transforms into a white

powder when "spun," or when the nucleus deforms, thus creating a high-spin state as the electrons shift in orbit and/or charge. Mention of this powder is first found in the *Egyptian Book of the Dead* and the *Papyrus of Ani,* by Wallis Budge, which is the oldest book of the dead, found about 3500 BC in a tomb. (See below for an explanation of a high-spin state.)

- Monatomic powder of iridium affects the pituitary gland and activates the body's "junk DNA," along with unused parts of the brain. (Junk DNA is a name for the thirty aspects of DNA that have yet to be explained.) As for our brain, we currently employ only fifteen percent of its capacity.

These elements are also the basis of levitation, currently used in the production of the superfast maglev trains that seemingly skim over the earth.

How do these magical metals produce such superhuman results? In a monatomic state, atoms lose their chemical reactivity and their nuclei reconfigure. The nucleus almost divides in half, into one section that is filled and another section that is half-filled. The new nucleus is called *superdeformed,* but in reality, it is "superamazing." It can now shift from a low-spin to a high-spin state.

In a low-spin state, the electrons fill the lower-energy orbitals around the nucleus before they begin occupying the higher-energy orbitals. Why is it called low-spin? It means that the lower orbitals are filled first. (You might call the low-spin state the lowest occupied state.) Guess what happens in a high-spin state? The higher-energy orbitals are filled first, rather than the lower-energy orbitals. If an atom has five orbitals, an electron is put into each before any pairing occurs, and we've now created a "high-spin complex." Atoms in this state are lower in temperature and can remain in a monatomic (*mono* meaning "one") state.

In this state, atoms can pass energy from one atom to the next with no net loss in energy. Remember our discussion of the zero point, which occurs when light is frozen? Even as far back as the 1960s, researchers saw that these metals, in a high-spin state or zero-point state, could pass energy from one high-spin atom to the next with no loss of energy! This process is termed *superconductivity.*

With superconductivity, energy—information that vibrates—can be passed from one superconductor to another, with no resistance and *no contact.* (Sound familiar? Remember Particle Bob and Particle Betty from chapter 4?) Under the influence of a high-spin nucleus, the electrons, which begin to spin in the same direction, turn to *pure white light.* They literally turn into photons. In this state, the element cannot maintain its metallic state. It begins to fall apart and appears as white monatomic powder. In losing their metallic nature, these metals also produce a magnetic field, called the *Meissner field,* to which we've already attributed effects like levitation. In addition, superconductivity has another side effect: weightlessness.

Researcher Hal Puthoff, director of the Institute for Advanced Studies in Austin, Texas, has determined that when matter reacts in two dimensions—such as occurs with monatomic metals—it should lose about four-ninths of its gravitational weight. For instance, a one-pound object if "spun" will drop almost half its weight. Where does its extra baggage go? Says Puthoff, the missing energy is now operating in a different dimension, thus rendering that part of the energy invisible.[4]

A relatively new theory called Causal Dynamical Triangulation actually illustrates the geometric structure of at least some of these space-time dimensions.[5] Through this latticework, energy transfers from one dimension to another. This means that it is possible for matter to "flash in and out of existence"—as does the soul at death.

Do we need to wait until death to disappear? More important—must we wait to access the knowledge that we would like to have *appear?* Not if we understand the role of the chakras.

Now Add the Chakras . . .

The ancients believed that the chakras held the key to in-body spiritualization and physical healing, and that metals played a vital part in this kind of transition. We know that our bodies already contain metals, and that certain metals can be toxic and life threatening to us. Small amounts—not to be determined at home!—may assist in the conversion to zero point and the elevation of self. Each chakric endocrine gland houses a specific transitional metal, which, when illuminated by zero-point energy, enables entry to the Plane of Light and a corresponding transformation.

Connecting transitional metals to metamorphosis through the chakra system is not a new thought. One of the classic esoteric manuals that first introduced this concept is called *The Emerald Tablet.* This book supposedly contains all the clues needed for alchemy, the turning of lead into gold and the mortal into the immortal. My own research—a blend of intuition and investigations of transitional metals and esoteric writings, including the Tibetan and Egyptian Books of the Dead, the Egyptian Gnostic Gospels, and Masonic secrets—would propose the following correlation of chakras to transitional metals. There is nothing scientifically solid about this proposal, but it follows both logical and intuitive lines of thought; more advanced scientific studies must be undertaken to finalize such an outline.

When stimulated, transitional metals activate our body's ability to heal and call in the wisdom of the Planes. This process is initiated by a new spin in a chakra, our "spinning wheels of light" that encode spiritual data for physical use. Ultimately, this enlightening process is activated when we're dying and works to help the soul leave the body. But it also works when we're embodied, inviting the following process to occur:

- A commitment to higher consciousness creates a zero-point spin in a corresponding chakra.
- This spin activates the transitional metal housed within the chakra's endocrine gland.
- It also animates the dormant connection to the related Plane of Light.
- . Our biochemistry shifts as the wisdom (and energy) of the Plane elevates our bodily functions.
- Our consciousness rises as we incorporate the Plane's data.
- Blockages among body, mind, soul, and spirit clear— and we begin to act like the beings of light that we are.

CHAKRA	GLAND	TRANSITIONAL METAL, RATIONALE
FIRST	Adrenals	IRON For its role in blood and carrying lineage
SECOND	Ovaries or testes	COBALT For magnetism and cancer curatives
THIRD	Pancreas	COPPER For absorption in digestive system and its role in these organs
FOURTH	Heart	PALLADIUM For its mythological association with wisdom and its affiliation with hydrogen, the core life element
FIFTH	Thyroid	QUICKSILVER OR MERCURY The "messenger of the gods"
SIXTH	Pituitary	IRIDIUM For its role in pituitary, dream state, and levitation
SEVENTH	Pineal	HIGH-SPIN GOLD For its role in activating pineal and use by ancients
EIGHTH	Thymus	SILVER For its role in conduction, boosting the immune system, and psychic activity
NINTH	Diaphragm	RHODIUM For its role in hardening platinum and achieving higher dream states
TENTH	Bones	MONTMORILLONITE CLAY As related to most elemental of functions
ELEVENTH	Connective tissue	INDIUM Which, along with salty fluids, balances and supports the entire body
TWELFTH	Thirty-two secondary points (These are minor chakra points, such as at the knees and hands.)	OSMIUM For its interdimensional connectivity
THIRTEENTH Highest Consciousness	None /All (There is no specific gland involved, but rather an integration of all endocrine functions.)	PLATINUM For its role in DNA, the cellular body, and activating all glandular systems to higher awareness

Imagine once again that you are an Egyptologist, and you have spent time exploring transitional metals. Through your exploration, you have discovered that they help the body shift to light, and you find that you've started mitigating the negative effects of life. You are beginning to experience yourself as the Great Luminary that you are. Core spiritual truths begin to make sense. You know yourself as the Buddha. You live as Nothing. You are the yin and the yang. As did Jesus, you can now say, "I am the Way, the Truth, and the Light"—for you are your own way, truth, and light.

Will research one day catch up to this ancient wisdom? We can only hope; but in the meantime, you can learn more by reaching out—and up—toward the beings of light that stand ready to help.

BEINGS OF LIGHT

When I die and they lay me to rest
I'm gonna go to the place that's the best
When they lay me down to die
Going to go up to the spirit in the sky . . .

Prepare yourself you know it's a must
Gotta have a friend in Jesus
So you'll know that when you die
He's going to recommend you to the spirit in the sky . . .

NORMAN GREENBAUM
"SPIRIT IN THE SKY"

A few years ago, my youngest son could not sleep in his room. He was only three years old and was unable to explain his fear. About midnight, he would trudge into my room and lie down next to me. As the night wore on, we would become entangled, and I found that it was I who couldn't sleep.

Sometimes I would drift to his room, but couldn't sleep there, either. The toys talked! As soon as I was ready to doze, Buzz Lightyear would announce his presence, King Kong would roar, or one of the many zippy cars my son loves would start to stir. Tired of being tired, I finally used my intuition to picture what was happening.

I saw the ghosts of several small children, each about age three or four. I observed each child as it wandered in, eager to delight in the toys. (We did have the best kids' toys in the city; it was little wonder that the just-passed little ones were attracted to all this fun.) In search of peace and quiet in my son's room, I called guardian angels to the scene and asked the beings of light to assist the wandering children "to the Light." My request was heard, the talking toys stopped talking, and once again we could get some sleep in my house.

Most individuals who have had a near-death experience report that they see beings of light, as well as the great White Light, upon death. Many people who are dying smile as they see deceased loved ones gather around them. Hundreds of my own clients discuss ghosts and unearthly visitors, experiences that are quite real. But who are the otherworldly beings that interact with us? In this special section we will explore this question, and then we will further discuss their roles in our deaths—and lives—as the book proceeds.

The Great Light

If there is any common concept of "God" across continents and eras, it is as a Great Light. Many creation stories stress the appearance of light, including in Islamic, Jewish, and Christian scripture. For instance, the original texts of the first five books of the Bible used the term *El* in relation to the Creator, which in the Sumerian tongue equates to "Shining One."[1] God is referred to as *El Shaddai* forty-eight times in the Vulgate version of Exodus, which has a meaning similar to "Mountain of Light," though the term was changed to *Almighty* centuries later. The words *U'rim* and *Thum'min,* used to describe the supernatural stones used in the Ark of the Covenant, mean "Light" and "Perfection," and in ceremony the Freemasons call God the *Great Luminary.*

If God is light, then so are we. This Great Luminary is the progenitor of the field of light that connects us all. We are simply smaller versions of the light, each of us "energetic representations of the original vast beingness." Through separateness, we gain the "diversity and self-knowledge inherent in supreme consciousness."[2]

We are all beings of light. There are also certain kinds of beings that are not "alive" as we generally think of it, yet can have a profound impact on us, whether we are alive or not. This is a quick overview of the spiritual beings that surround and interact with us, as well as what makes some of them "bad" and some of them "good."

Beings of Spirit

As we have seen in previous chapters, everything in existence is and has spirit, but not everything has a soul. Spirit is everywhere and "everywhen" at once. It only develops a soul when it individualizes and incarnates.

Here on earth, but not always *of* the earth, there are beings that have just a spirit, and other beings that have both spirit and soul. In fact, there are seemingly countless types of energies, beings, consciousness forms, spirits, and souls—all available to each of us on an as-needed basis. I'd like to introduce you to those I believe are the most basic, the entities that are most familiar to me.

My interest in the topic began when I was a child. My own psychic gifts presented me with visions of and interactions with various entities, including faeries, devas, angels, demons, and ghosts. This ability ran in the family: my dad's mother could see ghosts. She hated one house they lived in because it was inhabited by one. The rest of the family didn't like to talk about it; Grandma's uncanny ability literally "spooked" them.

My awareness and acceptance of the spirit world led me to investigate further; I read, studied, and made frequent trips to other countries. How do Costa Rican faeries differ from those found in Wales? How do ghosts interact with the living in Britain as opposed to Morocco? These were the kinds of questions that moved me to pursue answers in civilizations around the world.

My interest has been supported by my work with clients. Every day I "talk with" or "see" spirits, of every variety. A little girl might be accompanied by an angel and a deceased grandmother, a sheik from Arabia by a genie and a warrior he knew in a past life. The client is never alone—nor are any of us. Each of us is attended by several entities that are, in most instances, dedicated to our well-being.

My lifetime passion has resulted in the following categorizations. A partial list of earthly and otherworldly beings includes:

Natural beings: Including animals, birds, reptiles, plants, trees, and other living and natural life forms.

Elemental beings: Including the spirits of the major elements as well as the elements themselves, which are fire, water, air, and earth. These combine or reduce to create these additional elements: wood, stone, metal, light, ether, and stars. Wood, for example, is a blend of earth and water. Fire reduces to light. Stars are made of fire and air.

Faery beings: Including faeries, elves, devas, gnomes, getis (related to yetis, like the "abominable snowmen"), centaurs, jinn, and other nature-based life forms.

Planetary beings: Including the Blue People, Star People, and beings from other constellations and other celestial dimensions.

Human beings: Including ghosts, phantoms, ancestors, and other nonincarnate entities, as well as living people. Elevated human beings include masters, avatars, saints, the ascended, sorcerers (those who "work with the Source"), archons, forms, the Ancient Ones, the Watchers, the Wise Ones, and others.

Angelic beings: Including the archangels (called by many names in many cultures), angels of death, healing angels, *Nephilim* (or earth angels), Shining Ones, Powers, Principalities, and other types of angels.

(Note: Many of these beings are more fully described in Part II, The Planes of Light.)

Except for the human category, these beings exist as a spirit only or as a spirit with a soul. Many animals, for instance, surrender their soul, or individual self, to the greater spirit of their species. A cat, for instance, might retain his or her personal identity, and thus a particular mission; or it might represent "Cat Spirit." When a soul dies, it must evolve through the Planes of Light that fit its own type of grouping. But when a spirit leaves the body, it simply rejoins the higher spirit of its type.

Human beings, however, always take on a soul to enter the third dimension. Some beings go directly from spirit to human soul. Still others began as a different type of being and then incarnated as a human, thus "transforming into" a human soul. Still other souls start as a human and metamorphose into something else—perhaps returning to human form during a different incarnation. Some angels, who by nature are only spirits, incarnate in order to offer assistance. Faery or interdimensional planetary beings often do the same.

Souls often switch between types of being from one incarnation to the next, the decision being based on their spiritual nature, lesson plans, and desires. The first time I glimpsed this truth I stood upon a cliff in Wales with my dear friend Robert; I suddenly remembered "being the wind" after leaving a lifetime in which he and I had been mates. My experience of having "been the wind" explains why I heard singing in the wind as a child. A Peruvian shaman once told me that he had come here from the Blue Planet, and showed me a funny blue birthmark in the shape of a star. During a ceremonial journey he conducted, I was psychically transported to this planet and brought back information that he said was particular to that place.

Once you have a soul, you always have it. Spirit beings do not necessarily need to evolve; through their connection to the Planes, they know themselves as always connected to Source. Souls, however, are challenged by experience, especially when incarnated. As Betty Eadie, who has had a near-death experience, writes, there are "fluorescent light tubes in our bodies." When the light glows, we are filled with light and love. This light can be diminished, however, by negative experiences, such as lack of love or violence and abuse.[3]

The Planes of Light feed the "fluorescent tubes," or energy systems, within our bodies, keeping us connected and fed by the greater light. Groups of souls will access different Planes, depending upon their basic needs or personalities. Animal souls, for instance, will draw heavily upon the lower Planes of Light, which serve the natural world more powerfully than do the upper Planes. Incarnate angelic souls will tend to rely on the energies of the higher Planes, and therefore the higher chakras. To truly evolve through the "earth school," however, human souls must learn the lessons of each of the Planes. All of them add to the light that we are.

Not all souls choose to avail themselves of the Planes or the great White Light. Some souls simply do not know better. Life is so difficult, so painful for them, that they do not even believe in something greater. Some souls, however, consciously decide to rebel against the Great Luminary and all beings of light. These belong in their own category: "dark souls" or "demonic entities." What makes a soul turn against the Great Light—and indeed, its own light? And how does this affect the living and the dead? Let us examine these issues.

THE VARIETIES OF HUMAN SOULS

There are many possible forms a human soul can take. I am most frequently asked about *ghosts,* which are human souls that do not want to leave the earth. They separate from the body at the moment of death, but will not enter the Planes that could expand them back into their fuller ways of knowing. Many remain on earth for only a short time before entering the Planes; others stay indefinitely.

What causes a soul to refuse the White Light? Some, such as the little ones I saw in my son's room, do not know that they are dead. This is frequently the case with small children or people who die suddenly. Souls of people who were severely abused when alive often remain in a state of shock, and might wander the earth plane for a long time before they gradually awaken to their current reality. Some souls, for appropriate or inappropriate reasons, feel so bad about their lives that they do not want to "meet God." This is especially true of people indoctrinated by ideas of heaven, hell, a Judgment Day, or karmic retribution. Certain of being punished after death, they avoid leaving.

Other souls feel unfinished. Perhaps they left small children, a beloved mate, or other obligations behind. These souls usually remain on the earth plane until they feel it is time to leave. Still other souls follow a sense of spiritual purpose, remaining on earth without visiting the Planes, continuing as a human ghost or sometimes shifting into the form of another being (such as an element, faery, or angel) to complete their mission. As we shall explore in the chapter on the Plane of Rest, many souls linger until after their funerals or after they have completed the job of helping their descendents.

Phantoms are usually souls that linger in lower dimensions (which exist "underneath" the Planes of Light, and will be discussed in the next chapter) and are in rebellion while on a Plane of Light. They may also have difficulties separating from the earth plane. Many entity visitations are actually phantom related. The soul of a phantom, which does not occupy earth space, sends a projection of its energy or form into the earth plane. This soul might want to deliver a message or healing, but it also might want to frighten a living person because of personal issues.

Ancestral spirits are relatives who remain attached to their family lines. Most Eastern cultures revere the ancestors, turning to them for hope and wisdom. But an ancestral spirit might just as easily turn into a *haunting,* an entity that plagues a family line, stealing energy and causing havoc to avoid death and remain in power. These are often the precursors for *family miasms:* acculturated patterns that cause the passing along of diseases, financial and relationship problems, or addictions. Most of these haunting spirits attach to the living through *cords* or *codependent bargains,* energy lines that cut off contact to one or several of the Planes. All the books in my *Advanced Chakra* series address these and other energetic bindings and provide ways to release them.

Special considerations are made for certain types of souls, such as those who are aborted, miscarried, or murdered, or who end their own lives. This will be discussed in the chapter on the Plane of Rest.

All human souls have *guiding souls,* which are discarnate (have no physical body). Many are former humans. A birthing soul receives at least two spiritual guides: at least one is a once-human; the other can come from any other category. A human guide and an animal guide assist my friend Cathy; my oldest son is watched over by Christ and my deceased father. When I was a child, an archangel and a healing angel visited me. Deceased relatives often serve as former-human guides, although this position might also be occupied by a connection from a past life. These guides remain throughout life and are always present at death. Their job is to provide safety, instruction, mentoring, and direction for their subject.

Guiding souls are not limited to these two lifetime companions. As the well-known medium James Van Praagh explains, there are three types of guides. There are *personal guides,* which we have explained as human souls. There are *specialized* or *mastery helpers,* which assist with a certain activity, such as helping scientists make discoveries or painters create art. There are also *spirit* or *mastery teachers,* which I most frequently affiliate with an applicable Plane of Light.[4] We attract the guidance we need, when we need it.

Not all guides are invisible entities; the living can also serve as guides. One of my favorite clients, Cid, recently relayed a story proving this point.

In August 2007, the 35W bridge in Minneapolis collapsed, making international news. Cid had taken a different route home that day, or she might have been on the bridge when it fell. But she did *feel* like she was there. She felt her soul separate from her body and offer support to the construction workers at the site. The bridge collapsed utterly beneath them, but nineteen of the twenty workers lived. Cid experienced serving as a helpmate to them, among countless other beings she said were also present. As horrible as the event was, fewer than twenty people died. The number could have gone into the hundreds. Who knows how many other living souls assisted that day?

As we grow and change, so do our spiritual needs. The chakras actually activate in a sequence, starting in the womb and not truly finishing until we are fifty-six years old. Every time we activate a chakra, a doorway opens into the corresponding Plane of Light. A master from the Plane emerges, and we can potentially begin a relationship with it. In addition, other beings are called or attracted to us and help us through our life changes. During adolescence, for instance, a boy might attract several sets of guides to assist through this complex time. Later if, for example, he becomes a medical intern, his active guides might be limited to masters specializing in medicine or healing. Once he is practicing medicine, he might acquire animal or planet guides if he is trying to become a "natural healer," or a master of the particular Plane that is most apparent in his life.

As I've said previously, there are masters on every Plane of Light. Some of these have never been human. Others are evolved human souls who are still students or graduates of that Plane. There are many types of human masters—and not all of them dwell in the afterlife! The term *master* simply refers to a being that has mastered or excelled at a certain body of knowledge. *Saints* have achieved a unique knowledge of love because of self-sacrifice. *Avatars* are warriors who have fought to earn their wisdom. *Ascended masters* have fully enlightened their bodies through the Planes of Light while alive, and so "ascend" without dying. The Chinese *hsien* and the Jewish prophet Elijah fall into this category. Sorcerers are not necessarily evil; they are beings who work with the source. *Archons* are leader souls; when incarnate, they often gravitate to positions of authority. When disincarnate, they often reengage with their "councils," or the archetypal group they belong to, to continue to assist the earth. The Great White Brotherhood discussed by the Theosophical Society is such a council.

The *Ancient Ones* served the Divine in the original creation of the universe. They splintered into two factions, one good and one bad. They will be more fully discussed in chapter 17 about the Plane of Power. The *Wise Ones* carry important information about specific topics, and share this data encoded in light. The *forms* are beings (human or not) that have become so virtuous in their representation of a divine truth that they literally evolve into that virtue. The *Watchers* comprise the group that watches over innocent souls (such as children) and guards against evil. Many Knights Templar were originally members of this "secret society" of Watchers.

How do our guides communicate with us? That depends upon the guide. Natural guides work through nature, presenting omens, appearing in nature-being form, or working through the elements to provide input. The other categories connect through our own intuitive faculties, sending kinesthetic senses, verbal messages or tones, or visions. When visiting from beyond the grave—through a Plane or elsewhere—a soul often assumes the appearance most comfortable to the viewer. If someone's deceased father is "making a call," his physical visage will match his child's viewpoint. In all likelihood, this probably has as much to do with the memory of the living, whose brain automatically "sees" a figure he or she can identify with. Messages can reach us whether we are dreaming or awake, and they can also be delivered through other people and everyday reality. Pay attention, and you will notice the revelations constantly sent your way.

Fainter Lights

There are also dark, shadowy, or evil souls. Note my use of the word *soul.* A spirit is never evil. Even the vilest of demonic beings is attached to its own beautiful spirit, which will forever link it back to Source. But some souls refuse to open to the White Light. Light is sustenance, and lacking fuel themselves, they steal it from innocent souls. This is why I call them dark souls: they manipulate others to obtain light.

There are living and dead dark souls. We have all experienced being drained by another human being. Perhaps you meet someone for coffee. You are happy and energized beforehand, but you leave feeling like your energy has been drained into a black hole. It has been! This does not mean that your companion is "bad," merely that he or she is not opening to valid sources of light. Instead, he or she "borrows" yours.

Some souls, both living and deceased, exclusively steal light or energy. To accomplish this goal, they often use coercion or fear-based tactics to trick other souls into giving up their light. When we are afraid, our energy contracts. Instead of pulling more energy in through our chakras and the Planes, we actually release our light—providing fuel for dark souls. We also lose light when we are raging or feeling self-pity or blame; our light escapes our auras and can be used by negative people or entities.

Some discarnate and bodily souls have gone to great lengths to steal energy, committing genocide, torture, war, and other atrocities to create "energy batteries"—and sometimes in partnership with each other. Adolf Hitler, for instance, was assisted by a voice named Providence. Providence entered his life when he was a soldier in World War I. Once as he was eating dinner with several companions, a voice told him to move. Hitler did—just in time to escape a deafening roar. A stray shell killed every other member of his group.[5]

Hitler was considered a military genius. It's little wonder—the demon attached to him told him what to do. My guess is that the dark entity and its illicit companions used Hitler to establish the concentration camps. What better "battery" for light than that released by killing millions of innocent people?

Many people erroneously believe that they are guided by beings of light rather than beings of darkness. I still remember the frantic call of a mother whose daughter was levitating. The mother had allowed her to play with a Ouija board, upon which she continually connected with an entity called "Zach." On this particular morning, Zach had apparently entered the daughter, who was screaming obscenities at her mother while rotating around the room. We had to exorcise the demon to restore the girl's sanity.

Yet another mother called because her son had just committed suicide. She had studied New Age philosophies and thought her son's association with a guide named Zanzibar was "cute." But Zanzibar kept telling her son to cut himself and the dog. She found her son hanging by a belt in the closet.

I believe that there are dark and light entities of every variety. A troll isn't always bad because of its species; neither is an angel always good because of its heavenly origin. This point is an important introduction to the next one: some of us might actually carry the genetics or blood of these seemingly otherworldly beings, and so it's important to understand the power of free will. An example is the faery folk. Throughout Europe, tradition asserts that the faery bred with mortals, producing "halflings" of mixed blood. Suppose that this happened. These halflings then had children—and which of us might be descended from them?

Another example originates in the Bible, which mentions the existence of the Nephilim, fallen earth angels. Genesis relays that these entities mated with women, producing "giants in the earth." What would it be like to carry this bloodline? The Basque actually assert that they are progeny of these giants in the earth. And they just might be: science has discovered that the Basque carry certain unique genetic traits.

What if one of your ancestors was a Nephilim, another a faery, perhaps another a jinn or a demon? These and other factors, along with your soul issues, will emphasize certain chakras or Planes of Light as important for you. The crucial thing about these lineage issues is the attitude with which you approach them. There are no "good" or "bad" categories of guides—or ancestors. There is no such thing as "bad blood."

Beliefs—not bloodline—perpetuate fear and blame. Ideas such as those of hell and damnation for "sin" attract dark entities that can influence the living, the dying, and the dead. This is one of the reasons it is important to access the Planes of Light while you are alive. If you stand in the light, you can easily perceive what is dark.

THE EXISTENCE OF EVIL

Let me tell you a true story about evil. If you'd like, imagine yourself as a child sitting by the campfire, indulging in that time and space in which everything—even that which disturbs us—is real.

One morning I was preparing for a client who was flying in from out of town. Her messages had been cryptic. I knew only that she was being pursued by a "great evil" passed down through her family and wanted my help. I was in the bathroom putting on makeup in front of the mirror when I saw a big, black, winged creature behind me. It was huge, and evil, with bright red eyes. And this may seem odd, but I also found it beautiful—a translucent, glowing ebony.

I was not as shocked as I might have been. I used to see demons regularly when I was a child. They would enter my parents when they were angry and incite rage in our household. They accompanied each drink enjoyed by my alcoholic mother, and I believe they incited depression in her. But this being was different; he seemed a purer form of evil.

I told him to leave, and he smiled. Then he hurled a black thunderbolt at me, and the mirror shattered! A piece of it flew at my neck and gouged me close to my jugular vein. The cut bled, and it would sting, as if poisoned, for hours.

It took me a while to recover. Fortunately, I'm a mom, and mothers can't afford to pause for very long. While gathering lunches and backpacks—and wrestling shoes from the dog—I was able to reconnect with normal life. After I dropped off the kids at school, I took a few minutes to meditate. I knew I wouldn't be able to serve my client well if I let myself descend into my own fears.

When my client described the "vampire" that had been haunting her family for years, her description exactly matched the being I saw in the mirror.

How can these negative beings exist? How can perfectly good people get connected to, and worse, persecuted by them? Is there redemption for their kind? How do they really affect us?

Evil is anticonsciousness. No being is truly evil, for it always has free will. An "evil" entity—or person—is one that has chosen to steal others' light instead of turning to the Divine light. Some evil incarnates. The being I had seen, according to my client, was once a living relative and had transformed into a vampire. My client was susceptible to its machinations because, through her lineage, she carried its blood. This made her feel that she herself was evil. In this way, she had unconsciously allowed it to persecute her.

As I mentioned earlier, any of us could carry otherworldly blood, and some of it could be evil. But is this any different from being descended from a murderer, an abuser, or another sort of "demon"? On my mother's side there have been many famous and esteemed people, but also a horse thief and a witch. My client needed to understand that having a vampire as an ancestor didn't mean that she was a bad person—or a vampire! In fact, there might even be a redeeming grace in an inheritance of this sort. What else are vampires known for besides their bloodthirsty nature? They are extremely intuitive, long-lived, and have the ability to transform toxins. As my client looked for the good in the bad, she called forth her inherent psychic powers and gained a sense of personal power. She has not been persecuted by the invading entity since.

The vampire's "bite" before the mirror was a turning point for me as well. Because of that experience, I was able to face the "bad blood" in my own family, and unearthed deep and powerful gifts that I had never known were there. I never did discern the benefit of having a horse thief in my lineage, but the witch? As I worked with her story intuitively, I was able to access the amazing healing powers that she had used. I was then better able to perceive the causes of physical illnesses and could suggest herbs and other treatments that would help.

What's in your bloodline? Who or what have you been, in this or in other lifetimes? What entities have plagued or affected you? Journey the Planes, and you'll perceive answers to these questions; you needn't fear them.

CHAPTER 7

THE ENERGETIC TRANSFORMATION: FROM DEATH TO THE AFTERLIFE

Close your eyes, but keep your mind open.

ADVICE FROM A COSTA RICAN SHAMAN

I t was five in the morning, and I was enjoying a deep sleep when the door to the living room blew open. Though swathed in blankets, I felt cold air—and heard a voice whisper in my ear. "Tell her that there *are* angels."

I stumbled out of bed at seven a.m. and picked up the message my client Jane had just left me. She told me that her mother had died at five o'clock that morning.

Jane's mother communicated with me as she left her body, giving me a message to pass along to her daughter. Was that normal? What constitutes a "normal death"? How does the soul energetically leave its life cocoon, decide what to do next, and proceed with what we call death—and what the soul might call freedom? This chapter contains our final exploration into the energetic process of dying before we leap onto the Planes of Light, crossing the river of death while alive. Specifically, it outlines the four basic stages involved in death and dying, and includes a discussion of soul groups.

Stage One: Preparation for Dying

In most cases, the dying process begins five to seven years before death itself. The first change is energetic and involves the auric field.

The aura provides both protection and filtering, and regulates our relationship to the external environment. In order for the soul to most easily slip from life, the auric field must reduce in intensity and thickness. In the initial stages, and continuing throughout the entire dying process, the auric layers begin to evaporate, thin, and condense: imagine a sponge that dries out and begins to flatten. Colorations fade from bold to pastel.

The frequencies of the auric field also begin to alter, forming a universal harmonic tone. This tone, also perceived as a coloration or shape, will eventually align itself with the most appropriate Plane of Light. This is the Plane that has been achieved during the current lifetime. (Usually a soul will at least briefly revisit that Plane after death, although it might begin with lower Planes and then quickly ascend to higher.) Tones that do not match that of the achieved Plane might indicate confusion about life lessons, incomplete learning, or the presence of the energies of others.

I have heard this tone several times. The first was when my father was dying. While I usually perceive the supernatural through psychic vision, at his bedside during his death all I could do was sense and hear the otherworldly. There was a faint tone emanating from my father's body, which became stronger when he took his last breath. My sense was that his soul lifted from his body and hovered at the foot of the bed, at which point I heard a single, pure tone. At the time, I thought that my father had shared the gift of his song as he departed.

Later, I was visiting the house of a friend whose stepdaughter was dying. Once again, I heard a tone—but an altogether different one from what I had heard when attending my father's death. I had thought that tones might indicate the soul's personal harmonic, the special frequency that each soul operates on, but this time I saw a light connected to the girl's body. The tone seemed to correlate to the light, as well as to her soul. Later, a different friend put the pieces in place for me. A sound healer, she was playing music at her own father's death. She felt like the key was a critical factor in assisting him with selecting the right path out of life. *Aha!* I thought. The tone probably reflects the relationship between the departing soul and the Plane of Light. Since that time, I have perceived this connection and have been able to figure out which Plane of Light has been achieved (and is now open) for the soul passing over.

HANGING ON

The energies of others are only beneficial when they are loving energies. Love can help the dying person make peace with life—and with death. Unfortunately, the "love" of many friends and family members isn't always so loving. People often hold on to the dying, not to help them on their journey, but because of their own fears, neediness, or sense of incompleteness. They might actually pull energy from the dying person, or worse, place their own burdens on the dying soul.

My business assistant, Wendy, is also a healer and a grief counselor, and frequently talks about the latter work. Several dying clients have actually told her that they can't die because a loved one won't let them. One client said that she couldn't die because her daughter didn't want to deal with sexual abuse issues with the father. Another client said that he intuitively felt that his adult son didn't want him to die because he would then have to grow up and deal with financial matters on his own. I had one dying client tell me that she was ready to die but couldn't because her children would fight; she was the peacemaker in the family, and they didn't get along without her intervention. These stories indicate the kinds of unfair responsibilities we can place on the dying, whose job is to leave gracefully, not remain among the living. The real problem with these intruding energies is that they create conflict within the dying person's system and can lower the tone of his or her energetic patterns, potentially interfering with a smooth transition. Interference of this kind can also make it harder for a passing soul to select an appropriately high Plane for ascension.

While the living might weigh down the dying, sometimes the opposite occurs. One story stands out in particular. Joe was a forty-five-year-old single man whose parents had died years earlier within a year of one another. He was an only child. Since their deaths, he had been clinically depressed, unable to attract a romantic relationship, and afflicted with chronic fatigue syndrome as well as grueling nightmares. In his dreams, he was a soldier, killing without mercy. Joe would wake up sweating and feeling guilty about his participation in these nightly wars.

An idea struck me: what if these disturbances were inherited from his parents, rather than machinations of Joe's own soul? When someone dies, I have learned, the loved ones normally go through a year of conflict, illness, and depression, but not for almost seven years. To check out my theory, I had Joe visualize the locations of his parents' souls. He found them together, hovering just outside his auric field. Each was attached to one of his adrenal glands and pouring dark-colored energy into them.

I asked Joe to describe the energies being sent into him by his parents. His mother's energy was depressed and made Joe feel fatigued. He guessed that this was the source of his chronic fatigue, and perhaps some of his depression. His father's energy was heavy with memories of his involvement in the Korean War. Was this the origin of Joe's wartime dreams? Joe agreed that no matter what, he needed to release himself from his parents and their problems, but he didn't want to hurt them. Ultimately, Joe felt comfortable calling upon Sai Baba, his guru, who lovingly detached his parents from his body and sent them to the White Light.

Joe's symptoms ceased within a few days and have not returned.

Joe's parents hadn't wanted to make him ill. At some level, they thought that by holding on they were helping him. And Joe didn't mean to "get them stuck" either, but by allowing their attachment, he was keeping them from moving into the Planes. It's important to completely surrender the living—and the dying—or we interfere with the natural process of dying.

If the dying person willingly releases his or her loved ones, the aura now begins to thin. As it does so, the light from the Planes more easily saturates it. This zero-point energy attunes the chakras to the dying person's spirit, activating the transitional metals to create changes. (In the dying, these alterations actually increase the person's physical degeneration; the soul is choosing to leave, and so the spirit supports this decision. In contrast, when a living person makes a commitment to live more consciously, changes in the aura lead to increased light and spin, and the soul makes use of these changes to bolster health and well-being. As the years progress, the person becomes better able to perceive the various dimensions, Planes of Light, and beings of light.)

The aura gradually reduces to a thin band. In the spiritually attuned, it is usually colored white, gold, or pink, depending upon the individual's personality. White reflects purity of consciousness; gold reveals a powerful manifesting ability; and pink indicates a loving heart. If the individual is struggling with death or unable to make peace with life, the band might be dark, muddy, diffused, or even ebony-black. This doesn't mean that the person is "bad" or going to "go to hell"; rather, more healing will be needed after death.

During these last few years of life, the reduced auric field enables increased connection to one's mind, body, soul, and spirit. Dying is really a spiritualization process in which the spirit encourages the dying person to (often unconsciously) perform needed acts of self- and other-love, frequently in concert with the chakras.

The chakras evolve in tune with the changes that are taking place in the auric field. In the spiritually attuned, the chakras shift in hue from primary to luminescent colors. Each delivers a final message and encourages specific loving acts. As a result, you might notice the following kinds of behavioral changes during the years before someone dies:

- Message received through the first chakra: Makes financial reparations and assures that loved ones will be provided for.
- Message received through the second chakra: Increases in mercy and compassion toward others who have caused harm, finishes creative projects, and alters negative behavior toward positive ends.
- Message received through the third chakra: Sifts through beliefs, judgments, and ideas to attain faith and wisdom; teaches others what has been learned.
- Message received through the fourth chakra: Heals damaged relationships and serves as a beacon of love.
- Message received through the fifth chakra: Shares life truths with others, tells the story of one's life, and offers reparation for any cruel words or deeds.
- Message received through the sixth chakra: Sees self as the Divine does; communicates a vision for the future to loved ones and the community at large.

- Message received through the seventh chakra: Makes peace with the Divine and religion, acknowledges self as a spirit with a body, not the other way around.

- Message received through the eighth chakra: Changes any patterns that can still be changed and assists the family with doing the same. (Some patterns are so entrenched that it is too late to alter them, and so they must be addressed in the afterlife. The most changeable patterns include alterations in attitude, beliefs, and the ability to forgive. It's more difficult to alter deep-seated addictions, religious fundamentalism, and inherited prejudices.) Roots out evil or negativity at the core and claims goodness.

- Message received through the ninth chakra: Focuses concern on global rather than local issues. Works with spiritual insights and truths rather than greed-based concerns.

- Message received through the tenth chakra: Decreases reliance on nature and the immediate environment, even on the body. Sees self as a spiritual being and family members as the same.

- Message received through the eleventh chakra: Through spiritual alliances with guides and masters, serves as a force for good. Empowers change by being present.

- Message received through the twelfth chakra: Accepts self as fully human and forgives self and others for mistakes. Aligns with one's spiritual nature and begins to connect with the spiritual world.

ALZHEIMER'S DISEASE: VISITING THE SPIRIT REALMS

Alzheimer's disease among older people seems to have reached nearly epidemic levels. The truth is we're living longer, and an aging body is often susceptible to nervous system disorders like Alzheimer's, senility, or just plain forgetfulness.

Spiritually, Alzheimer's is a condition, not a disease. You don't "catch" or "cure" it or other senility-related problems. You exist within it. From my observations—and I have spent a lot of time working with businesses and hospices that house such patients—Alzheimer's involves increasing visitations into the afterlife, while still alive.

Several years before death, the soul of someone with Alzheimer's begins to slip out of the body to visit one or many Planes of Light. For some reason, the memory of these visitations is erased upon re-entry, but after a while, the soul spends more time in the afterlife than in life. My perception is that many of these souls are performing evaluation of their lives to date and doing healing work via the related Planes. In addition, many are evaluating the reasons for their problems in life. Besides revisiting their own childhoods, they often spend time in their parents' or other loved ones' pasts. By understanding the reason a parent was abusive, for instance, the Alzheimer's patient gains compassion and moves toward forgiveness, which in turn provides a healing for the self. Rest, Evaluation, and Healing are the first three Planes of Light. I believe that Alzheimer's patients want to move through the first few Planes so that they can leap into important and purposeful service immediately after death.

On an Alzheimer's ward, the psychic sensitive will perceive a prevalence of white spiritual energy. This indicates an abundance of zero-point energy flowing in from the "other side" to "this side." The doorway cracks open, and the souls of people with Alzheimer's might sally forth (leaving the door ajar so they can reenter). Angelic forces join them upon their return. Besides easing their own way into death, it may be that Alzheimer's patients are also sharing healing with the rest of us.

In a school essay entitled "As the Sun Comes Up," ten-year-old writer Lily Joyce Wujek writes: "Even at night there is light and even at day there is darkness." People with Alzheimer's might be seeing—and spreading—more light than the rest of us are, even as they occupy night during their days.

Near the end—perhaps a year before death—the Ka, or light body, gains in both importance and intensity. There are actually many layers to the light body, each of which serves as a prism to direct a particular Plane of Light or energy from the White Light. Western culture often fails to recognize or access the Ka, which provides protective, healing, and information-gathering services for the living. I often awaken the light body for fetuses or young children, as it helps them to retain connection to the Divine and guarantees spiritual safety. When the light body is fully open, it also ensures retention of important past-life or zone memories and access to all spiritual gifts. (Zones are energy-based spaces a soul visits either before, during, or after a lifetime. They are fully discussed later in this chapter.) Near death, the Ka takes over the thinning aura's protective role, forming a clear spiritual shield. This shield helps the dying perceive beings of light and deflect dark entities.

During the last few weeks of life, the Ka clears completely, enabling the soul to connect with the spiritual world. Hospice workers often report the musings of their near-death clients, who hold conversations with the loved ones or angels who have come to guide them through the dying process. Most typically, the dying are attended by their two lifetime guides, angels of death, and loved ones who have already transitioned.

As a dying person's physical health deteriorates, so might his or her mind or emotional functionality. However, if the soul is truly prepared for death, such degeneration is often matched by a growing surge in kindness, altruism, and good-heartedness.

But not everyone is fortunate enough to prepare for his or her death energetically. Tragically, some people are killed before their time. Others depart the body before their expected time, without warning. Insight into these special considerations of suicide, violent or sudden death, abortion, or miscarriage are provided in chapter 8 on the Plane of Rest.

POSSESSION AND DARK ENTITIES: SOULS THAT SCARE OTHER SOULS

There are certain times when we are more vulnerable to negative entities or energies. The most extreme of these are just before conception, at birth and at death, and prior to major life changes.

These time periods are all transitory. Our normal perceptions are shifting, as are our usual energetic boundaries. If you were an "evil" entity dedicated to stealing others' energy or light, wouldn't you take advantage of someone during these times? Negative or "dark" entities feed on fear—and death can stimulate fear.

We're all afraid of change. When we are alive, transition is like balancing on a teeter-totter; we're not very good at it, so we become even more frightened. Death presents a gigantic leap into the unknown. Sure, we'll eventually remember that we've "been here before," but our memories of the afterlife return only gradually. Dark entities prey on the fear of passing souls, perceiving fright like ripples of gray or shadowy energy. Sparkles of red energy shimmer within the fog, tiny particles of life energy. A dark entity consumes fear in order to obtain this life energy.

Why would a dark entity need to steal life energy? Because ultimately, life energy emanates from the Source. Having separated from Source, these entities have no choice but to get energy from elsewhere. The more intense a person's fear, the more life energy there is within it. Dark entities will use just about any means available—psychic messages, threats, and more—to gain this vital fuel.

Death presents a particularly rich "feeding time" for dark entities. The soul is very exposed at death. For example, the Ka, a protective mechanism, begins to part from the body. This allows a greater influx of light from the Planes and the White Light, but also creates space that can be filled by the dark. The soul resides more frequently in the heart, as does energy from the chakras and auric layers, inviting intimacy and the exchange of true love, but also calling forth deeper, unresolved fears. Just as beings of light begin to gather, chanting open the portals to death, so do the dark beings. The body, mind, and soul are exposed—to bad, as well as good.

There are many conditions that involve a negative entity influencing the living, dying, and dead. These include:

- Possession: Being inhabited by another entity or someone else's energy.
- Recession: Part of your own energy is held within or by something or someone else.
- Obsession: Someone else's energy is stuck in you; their thoughts or feelings are literally "obsessing" inside you.
- Depression: You are hiding part of your energy— a memory, a feeling, or even a spiritual gift—and it is inaccessible.
- Repression: Someone else's energy (or an entity) is suppressing or bottling you up, and you don't feel free.

The key to understanding the psychology of dark entities is this: they don't want to "see the light." They are extraordinarily frightened of it—of the Creator—believing that it will judge their cruelties and condemn them to eternal hell. Basically, they prey upon the dying to steal fuel for resisting the White Light, and will take advantage of any opportunity to get what they want. While an entity might roam the earth searching for any dying person, another could already possess a dying person and want to continue this parasitic relationship. Or one might desire access to a specific gift, and so "steal" it from the dying. The invader might send its personal issues to the other side with the dying soul, in order to avoid working on them. Or perhaps it might have abused the dying at some point and now feels threatened; consequently, it coerces the departed into depression or repressing vital issues.

Ancient cultures well understood the vulnerability of the dying, and often prayed for them. They made sure that the dying person was never alone, was surrounded by loving people, and was lovingly tended in a serene atmosphere with gentle music and soft light. Many cultures called upon particular beings of light to provide comfort, decrease fear, and help ease the passage of the dying. We can do the same for our loved ones, and ask that it be done for us.

Stage Two: Death

Now the dying person physically begins to die. The dying process is actually quite complex, and I've spent years putting together the following description.

Some of the information will mirror that found in the writings of near-death survivors. Esoteric texts including *The Tibetan Book of the Dead* outline many of the same dying stages that I describe, including a brief awakening before death, description of the soul's silver cord, and the appearance of several tunnels. Most of my knowledge, however, comes from my client work and my own meditative experiences. I have had nearly countless clients ask me to contact their deceased loved ones. Unlike mediums such as John Edwards, I don't always "talk to the dead." Rather, I am able to feel, see, and hear what they went through at death, and sometimes what they are going through in the afterlife. Time and time again, provided no knowledge about the cause of death, I have told a client how the loved one died, how he or she was feeling, and what the circumstances were, but also what occurred in the energy system and through the supernatural channels. Clients have usually affirmed that my perceptions described the situation they observed, and my additional, energy-based insights often paralleled the processes described in books such as *The Tibetan Book of the Dead.*

I also began mentioning my observations to friends in the hospice business. Many of them are also psychic and relay similar stories. In fact, it's common knowledge among nurses that before a death, the terminally ill suddenly reawaken, only to quickly fade away after that.

These are the processes I have observed:

- *A reawakening.* Before the body finally fails, most dying individuals experience a short-term spurt of energy. It is time for the final tuning. Are there last-minute changes to make to the will? Final words to speak? An out-of-town visitor who must be seen? An important holiday or a birthday present to wrap?
- *The failing.* The actual body shutdown might start weeks, days, or moments before the end. We know what happens on the physical level: weakness in the limbs, problems with the organs, pain or flaccidity, coldness in the extremities, difficulty breathing, faint heartbeat, perhaps a coma—and then the last beats of the heart and the final sigh.

  As the body fails, the energy system also collapses. The chakra energies converge and settle into a single bodily point. So does the auric field, which has already condensed and now wrinkles around the chakra energy, encircling it like a dark, rubbery band. This area becomes the exit point for the soul. Meanwhile, the Ka retains its protective role, but it, too, has thinned considerably and now acts more like a cloak for the soul than for the body.

The selection of the "way out" depends upon the personality of the dying person as well as the circumstances of death. In Western culture, most souls detach from the heart, the center of the human energy system and of love. Western values reduce to love, so many souls gravitate toward its corresponding energy center. Some souls might leave from an injury site. For instance, if the person has suffered from pancreatic cancer, the soul might pass through the third chakra, which correlates to this disease. If the death is from a gunshot wound, the soul might be startled into popping out of this site. Highly spiritual souls tend to depart from the seventh chakra atop the head. Then again, someone who has been addicted to money might exit through his or her first chakra, the one that manages security.

Before dying, the soul situates within or just above the exit point. It shifts to this site via the *silver cord*, a slinky, umbilical-like cable that attaches to the soul through the fifth chakra. During life, this cord links the soul and body. Souls get bored; earth can be dull. So they compensate for their earthly travails by traveling into other dimensions, time periods, and the Planes. You will have experienced some of its odysseys as night- or daydreams. At death, the silver cord will disintegrate so that the soul can make its final journey.

In the body, life energy congeals in "stuck areas." If you could film the energetic motion, you would spot pockets, gashes, and sparkles of red energy throughout the body. This red marks areas that represent incomplete issues. Continue to film, and you will observe that the redness gradually shifts into the exit point, where it collects as would boiling lava. This energy will eventually help "push" the soul out of the body.

- *The "Push."* It's time! The soul begins to free itself from the body. The emblazoned red energy erupts, burning away the silver cord and boosting the soul upward for its journey outward. Any still-physical zero-point energy spins into pure white light. Like dominos falling one to the next, body energy spins into the mind, and this cumulative energy flows into the soul. Still hovering between life and death, the soul "hears" a "train noise." This sound is reported by many who have had near-death experiences; it is the fallout of the instantaneous shift of energy between body and soul. The soul now experiences intense pressure, but also a sense of being helped and guided. The Ka now completely wraps around the soul, having transformed into pure white light itself. Here it will remain until the soul returns for another incarnation.
- *The Exit.* With a "pop," the soul now departs the body. NDEers often describe this phase as having an out-of-body

experience. Free now from the physical body, the soul hasn't yet opened to the next realms. Usually it floats for a moment over the death scene, looking down at the body it is leaving. It might quickly travel to loved ones, or visit a place in the past. Death angels provide critical assistance at this point, for they usher the soul into the next stage of dying by helping them see the real exit doorways: the tunnels of light. Some souls fail to respond to their guides at this point, risking that they will remain ghosts.

The Zones of Existence

There are four zones that a soul visits before, during, and after a lifetime. These are etheric or high-vibration in nature, and influence the soul's beliefs and relationships. These zones provide opportunity for souls that choose to disengage from energy cords or other harmful attachments, or to heal issues such as strongholds. Sometimes, however, souls create more dilemmas in these zones.

The zones are spaces that are accessed interdimensionally. I first became aware of the white zone through esoteric literature and teachings. Around the world, various healers teach that the soul creates a prebirth contract in a special space. Scientific research provided me a name for this space, and my client work has proven it accurate. I perceived the other zones through my client work. I perceived the gray zone as a blank and empty space we pass through before birth. I found that during regression several clients described this space, and independently of each other reported losing their memories in it. Esoteric literature, especially Hindu, discusses soul amnesia, and I found I wasn't alone in my discovery.

The black and red zones have comparable illustrations in other literature, including various books of the dead, but I first happened upon their existence through client work. I have tracked cords to a black zone and seen incredible changes in clients' lives after undoing them. I first worked with the red zone with a client who was clinically depressed. No matter what, she just couldn't unearth her repressed feelings or deal with her life. During a session, she slid into a space she described as red and discovered a myriad of stuck emotions. Other clients have told of similar experiences, unprompted by me and always with miraculous results. Who knows if there aren't green, yellow, or purple zones as well? Only time and further investigation will tell.

- *The white zone.* We visit this dimension before coming
  into a lifetime in order to create our life plans. I have
  named this zone based on research by Dr. Joel Whitton,
  a professor of psychiatry at the University of Toronto
  Medical School. Dr. Whitton conducted startling research
  based on studies showing that over 90 percent of all
  hypnotizable individuals can recall past-life memories.[1]
  In his own experimentation, Whitton regressed thirty
  individuals with a variety of lifestyles. All reported
  numerous past lives. The most dynamic discovery occurred
  when he regressed individuals into the space between lives.

  The subjects entered a dazzling realm. It was filled with
  light, and there was "no such thing as time and space as
  we know it." In this brilliant space, individuals created
  the plans for their upcoming lives, while entranced in an

elevated state of consciousness in which they were "acutely self-aware and had a heightened moral and ethical sense."[2]

Nearly all subjects recalled the reasons they had arranged their lives as they had. When given the choice to change their circumstances, nearly every person, now understanding the rationale for their predicaments, decided to keep things as they were. Upon coming out of the trance, the individuals who decided that they could learn their lessons in a different way experienced near-miraculous healing.

Not all esoterics call this space *the white zone,* but many agree that there is a space for decision making before birth. Here, we meet with our guides and decide our life purpose. We also preselect "destiny points," incidents that will happen, no matter what. We might choose our parents, children, life mates, jobs, and even accidents, mishaps, illnesses, and potential times to die, which are called *exit points.* We are very detached in this spiritual state, so much so that we often agree to situations that we'd never desire when alive. Lacking the strong emotion of physical sensation, a hardship might seem spiritually necessary and not as difficult as it will be when we're in body. The agreements made in this zone are often called *soul contracts.*

Once embodied, a soul can break a soul contract (or be on the other end of a broken contract), but this often presents emotional challenges. I've worked with hundreds of clients who couldn't release a former lover because they "just knew" they were supposed to be together. Other clients were certain that they were supposed to have children and never did, and couldn't get over "being cheated." Still others insisted that they were "supposed to" be rich or another gender or live elsewhere or have different parents, and couldn't get over the happenstance of their lives. Inevitably, these strong feelings of "should have" or resentments about what hasn't happened track back to a soul contract that hasn't been fulfilled. In these cases, I point out that soul contracts can be broken — and often need to be. Destiny is not to be confused with fate.

Clearly, this is an important zone for the living to visit as well, for we are currently living through the decisions that we made before birth.

- *The gray zone.* After leaving the white zone, a soul enters the gray zone. This zone is composed of near-empty space, although it is magnetic in nature. Magnetism erases electrical charges and information. This means that past-life and between-life memories are erased in this zone, creating a "blank slate" for the upcoming life.

- *The red zone.* This zone runs concurrently with the third dimension, almost like an etheric body alongside everyday reality. It holds all the emotions we did not deal with in our lifetime, especially emotions generated between ourselves and other people. After death, the typical soul will have amassed many denied and repressed feelings in this zone. These denied feelings act like an anchor, slowing the soul's progress through the Planes of Light. They can also draw the soul back for another incarnation. The chains to the red zone can be so intense that some souls choose to remain on earth as ghosts.

Feelings denied in one lifetime are usually ignored in another, leading to quite a significant buildup of emotions in the red zone over time. These often erupt at the wrong people at the wrong time, and can create considerable damage.

- *The black zone.* The black zone is available to all exiting souls, operating almost like its own dimension. In it, souls dwelling in the afterlife and on earth meet to review their interactions. This is the ideal place to search for cords, curses, and other unfortunate problems (see following sidebar). If they are not dealt with at the end of a lifetime, these unhealthy connections to other souls carry into the next incarnation or limit progress through the Planes.

ENERGETIC PROBLEMS

There are numerous energy-based problems that cause hiccups or stalls in a soul's development. These may occur within a soul, or between souls; before or during an incarnation; or even post-lifetime. Unfortunately, some of these issues linger and can pass from one lifetime to another. These are descriptions of the major energy issues:

Cords. Energetic connections will limit relationships and cause patterns. Cords operate like a contract between two or more people. The most common cord exists between a mother and a child. For instance, a child might agree to share her life energy with her mom in exchange for having her survival needs met. When the mother dies, the now-adult child might continue to feed life energy across the veil of death, becoming depleted in money, sexual energy, or even physical health. The mother's soul continues to feel obligated to meet the child's needs and neither can be completely free to pursue their journeys.

Curses. Energetic limitations put on one soul (or set of souls) by another soul reduce a soul's power and effectiveness and attract damaging circumstances. Curses often limit abundance, repel positive relationships, and create illness and tragedies. Curses are frequently the territory of black witches and voodoo experts and can be passed down from one generation to another and carried into new lives. One client of mine went into instant remission from multiple sclerosis when she tracked the disease back to a curse placed on the women in her family generations before. Her mother and grandmother had both died of multiple sclerosis.

Even everyday comments can create hexes. I had one client who, at age thirty, had never experienced a decent romance or a well-paying job. Through a regression, he recalled a mother in a former lifetime telling him he didn't deserve to be happy. This comment operated like a curse on his soul. When we lifted it through energetic healing work, he forgave his mother from that lifetime. A year later he was happily married and had just received a promotion.

Codependent bargains. These are agreements that make a soul ignore its own needs in favor of pleasing someone else. They operate like typical cords except that they are one-sided. There is a giver and a taker and no exchange of energy. One client of mine was stuck in an extremely codependent relationship with her husband. She did everything for him, including press his shirts, clean out his car, and pay most of the bills. He did very little. We tracked the pattern back to a past life in which she was the mother and he the child. Because of her negligence, he had died a horrible death. In her guilt, she had created a codependent bargain, a promise to remedy the wrong through self-sacrifice. When she forgave her past-life (and this-life) self, her behavior automatically changed, and slowly they began to mature as a couple.

Mental and emotional strongholds. A mental stronghold is an unhealthy bond between two or more beliefs, and an emotional stronghold is an unhealthy union between at least one feeling and a belief. An example of a mental stronghold is the permanent pairing of the thoughts, "Anger hurts," and "I am bad if I hurt people." If you are stuck in this stronghold, you'll feel bad every time you get angry. Repressed anger creates physical and emotional problems and keeps us from protecting ourselves against abuse.

Here's another example. Imagine that you agreed to meet and marry another soul during a particular lifetime. Your soul has the belief, "I must uphold all agreements, whether or not they are good for me." Because of this belief, you feel guilty and shameful if you don't keep your bargains. We're now looking at an emotional stronghold: a belief partnered with a feeling. You meet your long-awaited partner—only to discover that he or she is an absolute mess! Because of the stronghold, you marry anyway, and spend fifty years feeling resentful.

Lack of forgiveness. Ultimately, a soul hangs on to old situations because it will not forgive itself or others for decisions that were made. Forgiveness is the release of what was not, in order to open to what can be.

Stage Three: Traveling the Tunnels (or Not)

Having floated for a while, a soul is now presented with several tunnels. These are really *wormholes,* spinning vortexes of different frequencies that correlate with the various dimensions. These time-space vehicles can shift us between different spaces and times; they are vessels for traveling into the afterlife. The Hindus refer to these as the *wheel of life,* a term that has now been adopted by several cultures. They become perceptible when the zero-point energy has reached a certain level and the soul has at least partially incorporated it. Souls that resist them will spend longer in the third dimension, or might simply become ghosts.

There are two main exit tunnels, both of which are white. Each has several offshoots of various hues and shades. In general, the "less white" or lower tunnel has more dark branches, and the "more white" or higher tunnel opens to sweeter and sweeter shades of white. The dark tunnels aren't bad; their lower coloration correlates to the lower Planes of Light, dimensions, or frequencies. The differences between these two tunnels are:

- The higher white tunnel opens to the fourth dimension and above, as well as the corresponding Planes of Light.
- The lower white tunnel accesses the fourth dimension and below, and their related Planes of Light.

A soul may choose to enter these tunnels—or not. Having entered, the soul might cross the threshold into a Plane of Light—or not. Before we look at the tunnels and how they relate to the Planes, let's examine the non-Plane choices.

Non-Plane Choices: Where, Oh Where, Might a Soul Go?

A soul has the following non-Plane choices, upon death. These are available whether a soul enters a tunnel or not:

- Become a ghost.
- Remain in the third dimension and incarnate in another body.
- Visit the black zone and then make a choice.
- Go right to the white zone and plan for another life.
- Immediately pass through the "wheel of life" and reincarnate.
- Shift into any of the dimensions and remain there.
- Shift into the fourth dimension and then decide between tunnels.

A soul becomes a ghost if it chooses to remain in the third dimension without traveling a tunnel. A soul doesn't, however, have to retain the shape or type it was in a previous incarnation. It might die as a man, but as a ghost take on a butterfly shape. At death, it might leave the body of an old woman but transform into the form it had as a young girl. It might reduce from human form to wind or fire, or any other element.

Some souls transmigrate into bodies that already exist. For example, they might choose to enter a person, animal, plant, or another object in nature. If this is done politely, the incoming soul waits until the soul already occupying the body has departed. When a human soul takes over a living human body, it becomes a *walk-in;* the exiting soul is called a *walk-out.* Under the best of circumstances, this is a contractual relationship. The souls agree to the exchange, usually at a cost to the incoming soul, which agrees to finish the outgoing soul's karma. Some souls, however, are simply mean, and they kick the inhabiting soul out of its own body. The cast-out soul might now become a ghost. If unable to fully free itself from its former body, it might also become "corded" to the possessing soul for the current or many lifetimes.

Those who enter the zones instead of the tunnels lack the healing of the Planes. Future choices will usually reflect the worst circumstances of the just-completed life. For instance, a soul killed in a concentration camp might immediately enter an abusive family. A soul that died while being raped might incur the very same situation in the next lifetime.

Souls don't have to enter a tunnel to vibrationally shift into a specific dimension. If they are ignoring the tunnels, most souls self-select to remain in the third dimension, the most apparent earth dimension. The physical plane isn't located solely in the third dimension, however. The fourth holds a very strong physical presence as well.

The third dimension is a cube, or a box. Many souls choose to remain "stuck" in the third dimension because it feels safe. The fourth dimension, or time, surrounds and penetrates the box of the third dimension. Some souls die and then journey on the fourth dimension, often for indefinite amounts of time. This odyssey involves skipping between time periods and eons, visiting the past, future, and parallel realities. This process teaches perspective and the consequence of choices, but can also enable avoidance of commitment. Souls can achieve this dimension right after death, and also after traveling either of the white tunnels.

Other common nontunnel choices include entering the first, second, and tenth dimensions. The first dimension is a point and completely still. How better to "get to the point" of who you are, what you have done, and what you desire, than in quiet? If the first-dimensional soul is a positive and happy one, this time period can be enriching and helpful. If the soul is dark, violent, despairing, or horrified by thoughts of damnation, this space literally transforms into hell: a space of aloneness and self-condemnation. In all likelihood, the first dimension (when not affiliated with a Plane) is the hell described by so many religions. It becomes hell because the soul believes it deserves to be in hell.

Some departed souls directly enter the second dimension, a sort of "flatland." Narrow-minded souls love this dimension, for it reduces beings, ideas, and feelings to a flatline state. It is popular with fundamentalists of all varieties, who when living didn't challenge themselves with broader ideas. Probably, it comprises the "heaven" described by idealistic religions, where souls can "prove" the accuracy of their earthly beliefs and avoid consequences of the actions that stemmed from these beliefs—like killing others in the name of God! Souls can also enter this dimension for beneficial reasons, such as to attain the privacy and solitude needed to research or reflect upon a certain subject.

The tenth dimension reflects the natural world and the cycles of time and timelessness. Some souls, especially those subjected to trauma and violence, enter this dimension for rest and replenishment. They want to forget what happened, and might actually transform into a plant, rock, or star while recovering. Obviously, this strategy can also serve as an escape from reality and keep a soul from conducting necessary healing. Then again, why not "hang out" as a rock for a while and enjoy the scenery of earth? Time can seemingly stop to allow restoration.

The first, second, and tenth dimensions might also qualify as the Catholic idea of purgatory, a static state in which the soul rests and rehabilitates, uncertain as to where to go next.

You can access any dimension through any Plane of Light. There is a strong association between each dimension and a specific Plane, however. For instance, the Plane of Rest correlates to the tenth dimension. The Plane of Evaluation links to the first dimension, the Plane of Healing to the second dimension, the Plane of Knowledge to the third dimension, and so on.

Highly elevated souls might refuse entrance to the tunnels—they don't need a tunnel to get where they want to go! They usually transition into the higher dimensions. Refusal usually pertains to souls that have graduated from several Planes of Light; however, some souls turn from the tunnels or the Planes because of fear, anger, or higher purpose. An example is the Ancient Ones, a group of souls that frequently incarnate without entering a tunnel. I describe this group in chapter 13.

As you've seen, there are many reasons that a soul might not enter a tunnel or a Plane of Light. Here is a summary of these reasons:

- *Belief:* Many religions or belief systems assert the truth of reincarnation or of a heaven or hell. A basic rule of life is this: what you believe, you create. A soul often goes to great lengths to prove its ideology.
- *Desire:* Some individuals simply want a certain experience.
- *Fear:* Most common are fears of a judgmental God and the drive to avoid condemnation. Why go to "heaven" if you'll only get thrown into "hell"?

- *Revenge:* Many souls return to "get what's due them," acting like the judgmental God that other souls want to avoid.
- *Unfinished business:* Not everyone is provided a preparation phase before death or is ready to die.
- *Purpose:* Some souls are selected by divine or dark forces to continue returning, such as certain angels or demons.
- *Fulfillment of prophecy:* The Dalai Lama, for example, is a continually reincarnating soul. Before the current leader dies, he tells his monks where and when he will be born again, and returns with memories and knowledge intact.

Once in a non-Plane arena, a soul often forgets (or fails to remember) its connection to source, or sometimes, to its own spirit. If it detoured the Planes out of any of the negative reasons listed above, it probably also skipped around the great White Light or ignored its personal guides. Sometimes the resulting sense of aloneness prompts a soul to reach back into the living world and make a connection.

On a Plane, a soul can rather easily move around time and space. The guiding master often allows soul visitation to Earth and the living, especially if the visit invites more learning and growth. It's not so easy for a non-Plane soul to make this same journey, mainly because it is usually "weighed down" with burdensome thoughts and feelings. Any negativity translates as a lower vibration and acts like an anchor. These souls might then assume phantom form, projecting an image, message, or energy charge into the earthly world in order to make a connection.

A deeply disturbed soul might appear to the living as a frightening form, rather like the "monster under the bed" seen by children. Some souls create phantom projections *in order* to disturb; others, because of their own inner turmoil, simply appear scary. Some project directly into a lower vibratory being, such as a bird or a frog, and attempt to deliver a message that way. Still others gain considerable skill at projecting and are likely to look like they did when alive. In general, however, projections, versus true soul visits, are most likely to be ethereal, ghostly, or partial (as in, you might see only a head, not the body).

Stage Four: Entering the Tunnels (and Planes of Light)

The first experience of the fourth stage is presentation of the White Light.

Typically, a soul has already jettisoned from the body and floated for a while. It has been presented the white tunnels. The White Light appears either to help with this decision or as a result of the soul crossing into a tunnel.

Some souls don't experience the White Light, especially those that immediately reincarnate on the wheel, become ghosts, or directly access a dimension. The White Light might appear to help a soul decide whether to continue dying or return to life (if this is an option), or to go into a tunnel or not. If a soul enters a tunnel, it almost always meets the White Light.

Many NDEers report the presence of a being within the White Light. Usually, this is a spiritual figure, representative of the lifetime religion. Why wouldn't the Light conform to our standard, rather than insist that we adapt to it? With the Light's help, a soul now selects one of the two tunnels or continues its journey within one.

The Lower White Tunnel: Lower-Plane Choices

Most souls are adapted to the third dimension and its relatively lower frequencies. They are therefore most comfortable leaving the body through the lower white tunnel.

The "highest" vibration available through this tunnel relates to the third dimension and the fourth Plane of Light (Knowledge). Souls that travel and remain on this third-dimensional tunnel have several choices available to them:

- Direct connection to the first, second, third, or tenth dimensions. To refresh, here's how the dimensions correlate to Planes and chakras:

Dimension and Plane	Chakra
Tenth dimension: Plane of Rest	Tenth chakra
First dimension: Plane of Evaluation	First chakra
Second dimension: Plane of Healing	Second chakra
Third dimension: Plane of Knowledge	Third chakra
Fourth dimension: Plane of Wisdom	Fourth chakra
Fifth dimension: Plane of Truth	Fifth chakra
Sixth dimension: Plane of Peace	Sixth chakra
Seventh dimension: Plane of Momentum	Seventh chakra
Eighth dimension: Plane of Love	Eighth chakra
Ninth dimension: Plane of Power	Ninth chakra
Eleventh dimension: Plane of Charity	Eleventh chakra
Twelfth dimension: Plane of Mastery	Twelfth chakra

Thirteenth dimension (and above):

Illumination of Consciousness

- Immediate reincarnation through the "wheel of life"
- Access to the first, second, third, or fourth Planes of Light (Rest, Evaluation, Healing, Knowledge)
- Availability to the fifth Plane of Light (Wisdom)

The majority of souls enter the Plane of Rest for at least a short while, where they are bathed in natural energy for restorative purposes. If accelerating logically, they would then shift into the Plane of Evaluation, then Healing, then Knowledge, and so forth. Three of these four Planes — Rest through Healing — are similar in that they are personal Planes, whereas on the Knowledge Plane souls are encouraged to shift from an egocentric to a more inclusive focus. From this point on, the soul's evolution is devoted to learning that is abstract or universal. (In chapter 11, on the Plane of Knowledge, I describe it as a pivotal Plane, one in which the soul should shift from taking a personal to a more "other-oriented" interest in knowledge.) Many souls have transcended these personal Planes in between other lives, but revisiting them can be essential for healing from the just-experienced life.

The Plane of Wisdom is the only one available in the white part of the tunnel, although rarely do souls avail themselves of this entry point into the impersonal Planes. Most frequently a soul will enter the Wisdom Plane through this lower tunnel with direct intervention of the White Light or a guide. Probably, the soul enters the lower tunnel thinking it isn't qualified for a higher level, but a guide determines that it is. The other Planes are accessed through darker-hued off-shoots. These darker frequencies enable retention of life issues and learning, which will be worked through while on the Plane.

The Higher White Tunnel: A Choice to Fly

The higher white tunnel opens into the fourth dimension, or Plane of Wisdom, and higher. Souls that take this exit strategy have probably already gained wisdom from the lower Planes.

Upon entering the tunnel, souls can immediately access the Plane of Wisdom. To reach higher Planes, they journey through secondary white tunnels, each of which reflects with brighter luminescence. There is no true entry portal to the "Thirteenth Plane"; rather, this place of pure consciousness is a state that can be realized through readiness and intention.

As with the lower tunnel, a soul can spin into a different dimension or return to life via the wheel of life, whether visiting a Plane first or not.

I once journeyed through this tunnel when in Peru. It was a hot and humid night, and we were beginning our sacred medicine ceremony. We perched on tree stumps sadly lacking in cushioning while mosquitoes stealthily ventured under layers of mosquito netting and DEET spray. I had declined the sacred medicine, preferring to meditate on my own, and was in the starting ritual when I was energetically transported into the future. A voice in my head said that I was going to experience my own, this-life death.

I was pleased to see that I was quite old, if a little saggy and wrinkled. I experienced my soul exiting my body and my consciousness joined with my departing soul. I was rushed into a white tunnel, which I've come to believe is the higher white tunnel, and then hurled into a dark void.

"Where am I?" I asked. I did not get an answer, but my sense is that I was on the outer bounds of the twelfth dimension. A loving Voice talked with me, telling me that I could do anything I wanted.

I could perceive all the choices. There was the golden wheel of life, ready to spin me back. There were various spectrums of light, palaces of learning pleasure. There were other constellations, worlds, and universes to visit—but I could not choose. So I asked the Voice to choose for me.

I was immediately struck through the back of the heart by a black force, which then spun painfully inside of my heart. I would now interpret this as the compressed energy of my own karma and all the Planes of Light. Then, just as suddenly, I was in the All, a light so white that it did not have any color. I cannot convey the happiness I felt, bathed in this sea of light.

After a while—infinity, I thought—the Voice spoke again, telling me that I had to return to the body in the Peruvian jungle. I said "No." I was so reluctant to leave! The Voice patiently repeated this message. I continued to say no until I discovered that I was not going to win this argument. I then began to descend back into the world of form, gently rushing through the very same white tunnel from which I had exited.

On the descent, I could feel my soul-body getting denser and slower. I felt immensely sad and angry, and even more upset when the Voice said, "Because you are going backward through time, you will now know the future."

"Do I have to?" I asked. I did not want to know what was going to happen: who would live and who would die, who was honest and who was not.

"Yes," the Voice replied, "But I can dim the gift." I felt like a shroud of light was placed over the top of my head, and I slipped back into my body.

I looked around. My rear end was so sore, and I was sure that I had been "gone" for hours. No, it looked like people were just entering the first phase of their journeys. I glanced at my watch—and saw that I had only been on my odyssey for ten minutes!

After such an experience, who could doubt that the Planes of Light are accessible to the living—in or out of the body?

Soul Groups

Most of my clients, especially those who remember the afterlife, re-mark about the frequency with which their friends, loved ones, and enemies reappear. The book *Journey of Souls,* by Michael Newton, outlines various soul groups that constitute our spiritual family.[3] I believe that souls do move through life—and the afterlife—in clusters. Sometimes a soul brother plays the villain, other times, the rescuer. Either way, it is comforting for us to shift through time and space with souls we know.

I once had a client who felt all alone. She was studying to be a rock and roll singer and had a unique singing gift, one not entirely (or even partially) appreciated by the music industry, which expected a certain type of singing. Although her family lovingly supported her, she had never felt like anyone knew or understood her.

I suggested that we perform a healing I call "projection," which involves casting the soul into all current dimensions. I wanted to see if there were members of her soul group or original soul family anywhere around her. Immediately, she began crying. She perceived a group of blue-colored beings that communicated through tones.

She understood them, and they understood her, but very few of them had ever incarnated. She asked if they would continue to guide and speak with her, and they said yes, but then they offered her another service. They agreed to link her with living people of their soul group. Within a few months, my client met several people and immediately bonded with them. One gave her a singing job and another became her fiancé. Her life transformed when she could link with energies like her own.

I experienced the vital support of a soul group myself following my first brush with death, when I was only twelve years old. I decided to die. Life was no longer worth living, I had determined, so I told my parents that I was done. I immediately became sick with an undiagnosed "flu" and completely disconnected from the people around me. Then one night, I died.

There was no White Light or angelic chorus. Instead, a booming voice told me that I simply had to return — I hadn't accomplished my mission. I said that I didn't want to go, but I was forced by some invisible presence to begin the journey back down.

Along the way, I was drawn into a circle of people. They were all dressed in Victorian clothes, for reasons I couldn't figure, and I felt like I had suddenly come home. After I had visited for a while, a female member of the group took me by the hand and began to tour me around the earth. When we were finished, I returned to my body and my life.

I put the near-death experience behind me until a few years later. I had left home—I was nineteen at the time and had decided to live in Connecticut while my parents divorced. My girlfriend and I were standing in a cemetery behind a restaurant on New Year's Eve (okay, a bit odd, but teenagers are) when I suddenly saw a circle of people—all in Victorian clothing. I knew them immediately. They spoke with me, informing me that I had to go back to college, and shared ways that I could accomplish this financially. A few months later, I returned to my home in Minnesota and went to college.

Years later, I was in Peru studying shamanism, and I met a woman named Lee. We became friends, mainly because I felt like I recognized her. We began to travel together with a group. One year we were on the Isle of Man in the Irish Sea at Midsummer's Eve, and I suddenly knew why I had been so comfortable with her. She was the angelic presence who had guided me through the near-death experience and back into life! We began to recall past life memories together and felt like we had deliberately returned together.

Only a few years ago, the Victorian group returned. I came home late one night, alone, and could see the group in my living room. Even now, I recall the bald spot on one gentleman's head, the lush maroon velvet of a woman's dress, the tinkling sound of wine glasses. A spokesperson explained that this was my soul group, and that they had always looked after me. I asked why they were always dressed in Victorian attire, and they said that the only time we had all been alive together was during that era. We sat and chatted, and they informed me of much of what was to come in my life, and then disappeared. It is comforting to know that throughout my life I have been attended by a group of souls—some living during my own lifetime and others dwelling in the afterlife.

Souls weave through our lives. There is no true separation . . .

If our soul group is advancing quickly and appropriately through the Planes, the system works for us. We get into trouble, however, when we are ready to expand beyond the norm of the group. This problem is similar to that which occurs in a dysfunctional family system, such as an alcoholic family. If you do not want to drink anymore—or if you are ready to embrace spirituality, and everyone else thinks it is stupid—the family energy will attempt to draw you back. And you will want to comply, because souls (like people) enjoy tribal mentality. We do not like to stand alone, or worse, be punished for being different.

As you work with the information in Part II, keep in mind that your afterlife soul group is probably the same as the one that is around you in life. The choices you make now will affect you after death.

THE IMPORTANCE OF GRIEVING

I believe in the afterlife. Even so, I cried freely at the funeral of a friend. I didn't want him to die, and I was angry and sad about his death. Believing in the afterlife doesn't preclude the need to grieve. In fact, grieving is a very important healing process, one best explained through the wisdom of the Hawaiian culture.

The ancient *kahunas,* as author Max Freedom Long explains, were Polynesian healers. To them, the word for healing was *hoo-la,* which means "to cause light." You create light by restoring the natural relationship with the High Self, which I call the spirit.[4]

The kahunas thought that all problems originated from believing ourselves separate from our High Self. If we choose to, we can align with it—and open to its light—through a three-step enlightenment process.[5] These steps involve:

- Cleansing hurt and guilt
- Preparing the mind, as if for worship
- Performing *hoo-ola,* or "making life"

The graduate of step three earns the title *la-ko,* or one who "possesses Light."

When someone dies, or when we are dying, we naturally feel emotional pain. We might recall how the other harmed us—or feel guilty about the cruelties we inflicted. When someone leaves, whether through death, divorce, or some other form of separation, it's normal to first feel our own suffering. No one likes loss or separation; it makes us feel sorry for ourselves.

But where there is grief, there is love. Sadness, anger, annoyance—these and the countless other emotions that accompany change—show us that we have loved something or someone. We can only miss what we've cared about. If we accept our grief and feel it without judgment, we'll automatically open to the presence of love. Love washes clean everything. As soon as we acknowledge love, we have entered the state of worship.

To worship is to treat something or someone as Divine. It is to sense the Divine presence, even in the worst of circumstances. It is to trust that the Divine will transform something bad into something meaningful, important, and worthy. It is to believe in the afterlife, for if we — and all other transient beings — are divine, then we will continue to exist, and flourish.

Finally, we grieve — and love — by returning to life. You'll know that you are performing both *hoo-ola,* or making life, and *hoo-la,* making light, when you can again hear the birds in the morning and simply enjoy their song, when you can stop at a coffee house and order whipped cream on your café au lait — no matter the caloric damage. When you possess appreciation of the small things in life, you can appreciate all of the people and beings that surround you — and those that might not be physically in your presence anymore. You have become a *la-ko.* You have merged light and life and are walking the Planes while alive.

PART II

THE PLANES
OF LIGHT

In this section, you will be introduced to the twelve Planes of Light. Each has its own chapter. Open to any Plane, and you will discover the interdimensional wisdom that is available on that particular level of awareness. You will discover the challenges of each learning path, meet the masters who can help, and learn how to access the Plane's special teachings while you are alive. Travel through the Planes, and you will know how to die when you die—and live while you live.

After passing, some souls traverse the Planes step-by-step. When they are ready for another lifetime, they reengage the "wheel of life," incarnate on earth, die, and then leap to the next Plane in line. Other souls take a different route. For these mavericks, anything is possible. They might dance for a while on a higher Plane and then dip to a lower one, or jump backward or forward to a different Plane. They could take a "spa trip" to a lower Plane to recover from the intensity of a higher one. It's all possible.

Souls decide which Planes to follow (and when) based on both internal and external factors. Fear may hamper a soul's growth; then again, a flaming sense of purpose might quicken its progress. The White Light might encourage either evolution or rest. Work done during a particular lifetime might open an entirely new path. Each soul follows its own logic.

After journeying through each Plane in the following chapters, you'll be invited to conduct a special guided meditation to "locate yourself" on the Planes. This exercise is intended to help you figure out which Planes you've visited in between lives, which you might be enjoying currently, and which might be the best for you to focus on. For the most part, you'll know what to expect in each stage of your travels through the Planes. Each chapter will feature several basic sections, including an overview, and discussions of its chakra and auric field affililiation, key wisdom, structure or process, masters, potential challenges, and guidelines for discussing the Plane while alive. A few chapters showcase additional information to explain their unique twists and turns.

Finally, we'll explore the "grand finale," what I refer to as the "Thirteenth Plane," the place of pure illumination. There, you will be introduced to your own higher self.

May your spirit awaken to illumination and joy on the Planes of Light.

CHAPTER 8

THE FIRST PLANE: THE PLANE OF REST

CHAKRA Tenth. Located under the feet, the tenth chakra is your link to the natural world, as well as your historical lineage.

AURA Tenth auric field, also called the middle energetic layer or the etheric body. Surrounds the skin.

CHAKRIC COLOR Brown.

CHAKRIC GLAND Bones, specifically the bone marrow.

CHAKRIC ELEMENT Montmorillonite clay, used by the aboriginals in healing.

Overview of the Plane of Rest

How many times do we yearn for a place — or even a moment — of peace and serenity? The Plane of Rest promotes restoration and rejuvenation, which is often sorely needed after negotiating the stresses and demands of living and dying.

Many souls find respite on this Plane immediately after death. It is usually perceived as an idyllic garden, similar to the Garden of Eden described in the Bible. This Plane presents itself to us as the natural world, filled with nature's elements and wildlife, but in energetic rather than physical form. Where better to rest and rehabilitate but in nature?

Some souls skip the Plane of Rest entirely. Others use it as a vacation resort, visiting it to recover from work on the higher Planes. Still others linger there for centuries. It is available to all deceased souls, for rest is always important. No matter the reason for the visitation, its essential wisdom is the same. On this Plane, a soul receives the blessing of restoration—and is taught how to restore itself, a skill we need to learn in life as well as in death.

The Affiliation with the Tenth Chakra and Auric Field

The tenth chakra connects us to nature and our heritage, enabling healing and restoration through the elements. There are four basic elements—fire, water, earth, and air. These create six additional elements: stone, wood, metal, ether, light, and star. Elements enter our physical bodies through the bone marrow, the tenth chakra endocrine gland (technically, bone marrow isn't a gland; it does produce blood, which carries hormones throughout the body). These elements are processed according to our individual needs and genetic programming. Bones are crystalline in form, channeling the energy of light so as to correctly activate the DNA.

Bone marrow is where blood cells are produced. According to many Eastern medicine traditions, the blood carries our life spirit, as well as our ancestral inheritance. Montmorillonite clay contains tiny crystalline particles, and thus mirrors the function of bones to activate our "spiritual DNA"—the genetics that support our spiritual destiny—while healing any legacy from our forebears that does not match our unique self.

The tenth auric layer sits just atop the skin. Also called the *middle energetic layer* or the *etheric body,* it repels harmful energies and accepts beneficial ones. This layer is programmed by our heritage, and as a result often fails to provide us with the defense we really need. All the damage incurred in life—physical, emotional, mental, and spiritual—is transferred to the soul at death. So what could be more important immediately after dying than the elemental healing the Plane of Rest provides?

The Qualities of the Plane of Rest

The garden on the Plane of Rest is composed of the same properties present in gardens on earth, with two main differences. All elements run at a higher vibration than on earth, and they are also fully conscious.

In the special section on the beings of light, you learned about natural and star beings, as well as elements. These and additional natural beings inhabit the Plane of Rest. Many of them were once earthbound. Some have permanently transcended to the Plane of Rest; others serve on this Plane and then return to earth. A gnome might tend to a depressed soul's needs on this Plane while a faery repairs the energetic arm of someone who lost one in life. In return, the visiting soul shares its own special light and divinity with its natural helpers. This Plane is a true model for the best way to live on earth.

The Wisdom of the Plane of Rest

The Plane of Rest has two purposes. The first is to provide necessary repair and restoration. But there is a higher goal: to teach the soul how to rest.

Life is overly hectic, and stress is at the root of so many of life's problems. We must know how to slow down and rejuvenate, how to become one with nature and with our own natural self. A soul therefore "graduates" from the Plane of Rest when it has accomplished the following:

- Has been restored
- Accepts the importance of self-restoration and has learned how to do it

The Masters on the Plane of Rest

One's lifetime guides and an angel of death typically attend the departing soul. At least one of these helpers ushers the soul to the gates of the garden, where masters of the Plane take over. Who or what might you encounter there? Look around. Get outside. Breathe in the air, enjoy the colorful petals of a flower, or pet a dog. These are examples of masters found on earth — and they are recognized as such on the Plane of Rest. Typical masters on this Plane include:

- Spiritual representatives from the soul's religion or spiritual ideology.

- Angels, especially those from the healing teams of light, which are special groups of angels devoted to healing the living and souls in the afterlife.
- A deceased relative who loved you during your life.
- A trusted friend or relative from a past life. (This occurs mainly for advanced souls who are ready to quickly remember and assimilate their past-life memories and abilities.)
- Natural spirits that always dwell on the Plane of Rest, especially those related to animals, birds, and reptiles, trees and plants, the faery realms, the planetary spheres, and the elements themselves.
- Natural beings that served as guides during the just-experienced lifetime. On earth, most native groups perform ceremonies to meet their *totems,* sometimes called *natural guides, power animals,* or *companion friends.* These are natural beings that call forth our special powers, provide teaching and instruction, serve as healers or diviners, or act as our friends.
- A student of a higher Plane of Light who is learning through service on this Plane. The most qualified are attendants from the Planes of Healing, Love, and Charity.

Upon entering the Plane of Rest, every soul is greeted by at least one master, who serves as a companion and guide throughout the stay. His or her first role is to tend to any disturbance or shock that has been carried in from life. This master usually performs the task by using natural elements to soothe, heal, and repair the soul. Here are the functions and types of beings associated with the elements:

Fire: Transforms, eliminates, and destroys toxic ideas and materials. In the garden, fire is available from the sun, flames, red or fiery-colored flowers, or beings that use fire such as dragons, fireflies, star dwellers, and many reptiles (including lizards and snakes).

Air: Distributes and releases ideas and thoughts, "blows away" dysfunctional beliefs, and activates spiritual truths and memories. In the garden, air is present in the wind, breezes, storms, and interactions with air beings, including birds and airborne members of the faery realm.

Earth: Heals, repairs, protects, and rebuilds wounded tissue. In the garden, it is formed from soil, rocks, trees, plants, and carried by beings of the earth, including animals, sylphs, elves, gnomes, and dwarves.

Water: Soothes, cleanses, purifies, and formulates intuition. In the garden, water is present in all bodies of water, including lakes, streams, and seas; in constructions such as fountains; and in water beings such as dolphins, fish, and whales, as well as faery entities such as mermaids, dyads, and water faeries.

Once the soul has been soothed, the master then eases the soul into the second stage of development, which is to learn how to restore the self. It is *pleasant* to be tended by others, but it is *necessary* to know how to tend the self.

We all have the ability to pacify, renew, and balance ourselves. If we do not become skilled at doing this when alive, we probably will not know how to do it in the afterlife. At the very least, the master on the Plane of Rest will teach a soul how to call forth and use the four main elements.

Potential Challenges

As with any process, there are potential problems in negotiating the Planes. While a soul cannot get a "failing grade" on a Plane, it can be unsuccessful at accessing and applying the knowledge that has been made available to it. If a soul does not learn how to self-restore on the Plane of Rest, it will return to life with the following problems:

- *Inability to distinguish between life and death.* People with this issue often feel "out of it": numb, apathetic, or mentally muted.
- *Lack of self-care capacity.* In life, this leads to dependency, codependency, fear of being alone, and lack of self-value.
- *Disconnection from nature.* Indications include dissociation, environmental sensitivities, inability to feel or care for the body, and problems with money, housing, or other basic needs.
- *Anxiety.* If we cannot nurture or nurse ourselves, we will be frightened of challenges — both real and imagined. Anxiety is fear of the future, the belief that one cannot deal with something that might happen. It is really the fear of the unknown.

- *Depression.* Toxic feelings, thoughts, and poisons build up over time. Unless we cleanse and nourish ourselves, the past will block us in body, mind, and soul. The consequence is depression, which involves being stuck in the past, and the resulting symptoms of heaviness, disease (or ill-at-ease), emotional repression, and exhaustion.

The Plane of Rest — For the Living

You can achieve and receive from this Plane while you are alive. This will ensure you a lifetime—and an afterlife—that is calm and balanced. Here are a few methods for walking the Plane of Rest today:

- . *Meditation.* Calms and encourages a restful mind.
- *Prayer.* Invites restoration from spiritual sources.
- *Contemplation.* Basking in nature or spiritual energies promotes effortless renewal.
- *Water works.* Practice listening to your intuition, get a fountain, listen to or sit near the water, or ask for the help of the water beings. Dwell in the current of your feelings; they emanate from the same source as does water.
- *Air ways.* Keep learning! Air represents ideas and concepts. Fill your mind with the food of philosophy. Replenish your breath: breathe in to the count of four and then hold for the count of four, then release to the count of four. Do this four times at a sitting, four times a day. Learn how to listen to the wind—it carries the songs of angels.

- *Earth matters.* Spend time outside, grow a garden, or put plants in your house. Learn native practices such as interpreting the signs of nature, and identify your totem animal. Spend time with trees and other earth elementals.
- *Fire walking.* Get ten minutes of sun every day. Follow your passions; they represent your inner fire. Light candles when performing ceremonies; write down your problems in a letter and then burn it; deal with your anger. Learn forgiveness, the overall key to restoration.
- *Energetically.* Concentrate on the color brown or use a brown stone or piece of wood to charge your first chakra for rest. Use clay topically to draw out negativity. (As with all transitional metals, never actually imbibe or treat yourself with it. This can be highly dangerous or lethal. It is enough to work with intention.)

WHEN SOULS NEED MORE REST

Certain souls are treated with great care in the Plane of Rest, especially those who have had short or traumatic lives or sudden, harrowing deaths. These souls often arrive on the Plane of Rest in shock and require gentle treatment. So do suicide victims, who are not considered "murderers" (as some religions would state), but rather victims of horror. Often, the very young—infants, children, or aborted or miscarried fetuses—do not even know that they are dead, and need the special care available only on the Plane of Rest.

For these souls, the Plane of Rest is like a hospice. When the soul arrives, soothing angels of healing spin it into a dreamlike state, equivalent to a morphine or sacred medicine trance. Suicide or abuse victims are often so distressed that their guides must use an amnesia-producing mist. Next, the attendants remove all horrific memories, storing them in a separate place. They then ensure that the Ka is tightly woven around the soul, which they rock into a benign sleep.

Over time, the challenging memories are reintroduced; you could say that they are sung as lullabies into the sleeping soul. Healing messages are interwoven with these recollections to stave off secondary trauma.

When the soul is deemed able to return to consciousness, it continues to be attended by healing angels of light, as well as another host of helpers. Many of the guides are similar to therapists and are students or graduates of the Planes of Charity or Love. Masters from the Planes of Evaluation and Healing are often present when memories are triggered, and former suicide victims often attend to souls that left through suicide. All of these are able to work elementally, and can call upon any of the natural guides for assistance.

In many ways, this deep, healing state could be compared to the Catholic idea of purgatory (as can many of the lower dimensions). It presents as suspended animation. Prayers from the other side are treated like letters from home, lovingly inserted into the comatose soul, which is gradually exposed to more and more love—from the living and the guides. Sometimes, a soul transcends all the personal Planes while in this state. These include Rest, Evaluation, and Healing. The fourth, the Plane of Knowledge, is a pivotal

Plane, inviting the shift from ego to other. Souls enter it for personal development but only exit when they are able to take a more global and universal view of reality. Rest, evaluation, healing, and self-knowledge (in this case, an assessment of what one already knows) are more easily experienced in stillness.

Special care is also provided to the souls of deceased infants and children. These are often carried onto the Plane by matronly angels and initiated into a nursery center in the Plane of Rest. There, they are often "raised" into adulthood, developing just as they would in life. Many times, I have been visited by these maturing souls, who appear during intuitive sessions to talk with their living mothers and fathers. The still-growing children appear and sound just as they would if alive; if they would now be five years old, they look five. At some point, the child-soul develops enough to begin climbing the Planes of Light, although at this point, he or she usually skips the lower Planes and catches up to the Planes achieved after a previous lifetime.

The masters often encourage an ongoing relationship between these baby-souls and their living loved ones, as well as with any other souls that passed at the same time. With the living mother in particular, this connection is assured through a golden cord, a shining stream of light that keeps the two bonded. This cord is disallowed, however, if the parent did not want or love the child, or if the ongoing bond would be unhealthy for either party.

What about abortion or miscarriage? Some abortions were preordained, usually by souls who only needed to come into a body for a short amount of time. This is common for highly advanced masters, avatars, or even angels that want a taste of the human experience. Some souls did not want to be aborted. These are immediately transported to the Plane of Rest, where they await a new set of parents or a second chance at returning to the first set.

There are many reasons for miscarriage. At least one in four pregnancies results in miscarriage because of a problem with the embryonic body. This is a fairly benign situation; the souls affected by it usually reside briefly on the Plane of Rest and then return for another try at incarnation. If the miscarriage resulted from a serious disturbance, such as rape or abuse, the soul visits the Plane of Healing (and sometimes the Plane of Evaluation, in order to forgive any transgressor) before returning.

The topic of twins is an interesting one. Many pregnancies involve the conception of twins, but one of the two is lost. This is becoming even more widespread with the increased use of fertility treatments. I have worked with numerous clients who remember a "ghost twin" and insist that this soul remains in contact, sometimes to help, other times to harm.

Some souls enter a twin body only briefly and then die in order to remain connected to the living soul. These remain in the third dimensions, serving as guides or helpers. Raised by the mother-angels on the Plane of Rest, they continue to age as if alive. Other ghost twins are more demonic in nature, seeking to steal the life from the living twin. Some even try to drive the living twin's soul from its body so that they can take over. These "negative" souls antagonize through bad dreams and negative thoughts, and by suggesting distorted behaviors.

I had one client with a ghost twin who could not sleep at night; the ghost twin would chant cruelties at her during sleep. When she tried to disconnect from it, it began causing traffic accidents—one month she had four such accidents. These negative souls are true ghosts. Having never entered the Planes of Light, they must be sent to the light with caution and love. Few make it onto the Planes on their own; their fear and self-delusion is too great, as is the accrued guilt from their "bad behavior." Spiritual guides never give up on their subjects and consistently create situations that will help these stuck souls get to the Planes. If you as a living person feel compelled to help an errant soul to the other side, make sure you engage spiritual help.

There is an interesting question regarding twins: do identical twins have one or two souls? Either may be the case. Sometimes a single soul splits in order to learn certain lessons, usually centered on intimacy with the self. Sometimes two souls select identical bodies to focus on lessons about connection. The easiest way to discern if an identical twin is one or two souls is to compare personalities. Distinctive personalities often indicate two different souls, "identical" personalities, the same soul.

CHAPTER 9

THE SECOND PLANE: THE PLANE OF EVALUATION

CHAKRA First. Located in the groin, this chakra regulates our safety and security issues.

AURA First auric field, which includes the skin and just above the skin. This auric field serves as our primary defense against physical marauders such as bacteria, would-be attackers, and the elements.

CHAKRIC COLOR Red.

CHAKRIC GLAND Adrenals.

CHAKRIC ELEMENT Iron, which carries our "strength."

Overview of the Plane of Evaluation

To evaluate means to assess or to calculate. We usually think that evaluations are negative or judgmental. They aren't. The goal of a soul evaluation is to understand our own pricelessness.

The Plane of Evaluation presents a life review, usually limited to the life just experienced. The mechanics of a life review are simple but challenging, and involve at least these basics:

- Examination of significant life events
- Review of others' experiences, so we can understand how we affected them
- Assessment of life events as an "objective observer," gaining the ability to see all sides of the story from a Divine perspective

The ultimate goal of the Plane of Evaluation is for the soul to assume self-responsibility, with compassion for self and others.

Some souls jump immediately to this Plane, skipping the Plane of Rest. Most souls journey to this Plane after every lifetime, unless they have thoroughly reviewed their life before death.

Every life holds value—we do not review our lives to condemn our choices or actions, but rather to gain empathy and thus soften our souls for further growth.

The Affiliation with the First Chakra and Auric Field

The first chakra and auric field regulate our existence and issues of safety and security. During our lifetimes, these energy organs keep us alive, managing energies to manifest our vital needs. The corresponding transitional metal—iron—represents our strength, character, and independence. Iron symbolizes our ability to be vital and lead rich lives.

A lifetime of challenges can sap our strength. By the time we're adults, we feel guilty. Maybe we haven't fulfilled our destiny or lived up to our own self-image. When we're alive, this negative self-evaluation saps our essential energy and encourages illness. On the

Plane of Evaluation, we take a look at the issues that "zapped" us. The usual culprit is being judgmental.

The Wisdom of an Evaluation

Most NDEers report undergoing a life review. Their life reviews are essentially the same as the evaluations on this Plane. The NDEers are surprised by what the review shows them. They find that the things that were really important about their lives, the key events, were the unexpected ones. They weren't the first job, marriage, or divorce. Instead, they included a grandmother's smile, the happiness of a well-tipped waitress, the burst of a brilliant sunset. And sometimes, the most terrifying or traumatic events were the most significant of all.

On this Plane, the soul learns to examine life (and itself and other souls) from a Divine perspective. Think of life as a tapestry. The pretty picture on the front is created by the meandering, sometimes knotted and ugly threads on the back. *Every* experience on the back is necessary to form the beautiful composition on the front.

The Structure of a Life Review

A thorough life review encompasses the following:

- *A walk through the lifetime, including in utero.* Most of us became "stuck" at a certain age and must be freed to move forward.

- *A review of others' inner experiences of us.* Extra time is taken with people we hurt, or those who hurt us. (Further healing will occur on the Plane of Healing.)
- *A glimpse into what "might have become."* Don't you often ask yourself what might have been? Some souls hold on to guilt or pain unless given a look into the crystal ball—visions of the future as it *will be* on earth, or as it *could have been* if they were still alive.
- *If necessary, visits to the four zones of existence, as described in chapter 7.* Zones are often reviewed during an in-depth life evaluation, and any necessary healing is then performed on the Plane of Healing.

The Masters of the Plane of Evaluation

There are many helpers and masters on the Plane of Evaluation. They include:

- *At least one of the two lifetime guides:* He or she was a witness to it all.
- *Angels:* The most frequent angel guides at this level are the cherubim. Cherubim are time travelers. They have multiple wings and dozens of eyes, and can therefore travel anywhere and see everything.
- *Religious figures from the just-experienced religion.*
- *Masters from other Planes:* They serve as guides for their own learning.

Potential Challenges

We cannot really "leave" the Plane of Evaluation until we have learned compassion. And the opposite of compassion is shame.

Shame comes from believing there is something wrong with us. It is an actual energy, often appearing like a gray blob or cloud in the body or soul. Most worldly institutions and families excel at producing shame, insisting that we are "weird" or "wrong." Thinking that there is something wrong with us, we might avoid facing our wounds, problems, or behaviors — or even embracing our Divine gifts. Shame also keeps us from empathizing with others' feelings. We think we'll feel worse if we embrace the ways we've hurt others.

SENSELESS DEATHS

One of the most challenging issues is the question of a senseless death.

Many people hate death because they've lost loved ones for no seeming purpose. Suicide, the death of a child, victims of drunk drivers — these and many other deaths just make no sense. They make us question the existence of a god, or at least the value of such a being. They make us hate our fellow human beings, especially those that perpetuate great wrongs.

These same issues can confound the soul in the afterlife: "Why did I die? I wasn't ready!" We can imagine being plagued by our own protests, and wanting answers.

I had just started my intuitive practice twenty years ago when a client asked about a death that was overwhelmingly insane and awful. He and his four-year-old daughter were driving to church when a drunk driver—who had been out all night—smashed into them. My client, John, watched as his daughter's small body unhinged from the child seat in the back of the car, sailed through the front windshield, and bounced off the hood. We both sobbed as he told his story, and I wondered how I—or even God—could ever comfort a man who had witnessed such a tragedy. I turned the session over to the Divine.

I began to experience everything the little girl had gone through, from the moment of impact to being greeted by a great White Light. It was as if I were she. I listed thoughts and described contusions on "my body." John confirmed that each of these sites actually was injured in the accident. I described separating from the body and the angels who were there. I shared information and messages of love, using language and special terms that only the little one could have known. And in the end, John, knowing that his daughter was "with the angels," gained a sense of peace.

The beauty of the afterlife doesn't compensate for the ugliness of abuse or the trauma and senselessness of certain deaths, but it does provide a contrast. The world is transient. Everything and everyone passes away, but some deaths are more ravaging than others. The best advice I was ever given about dealing with the horror of a senseless death was from the oncologist attending my dad's death.

My father was dying, and my aunt was crying. She was also mad. My aunt couldn't understand why God would do this to her "little brother." If God could inflict this kind of pain on his children, why would he even bother to provide a heaven? The doctor looked at her and said, "The problem is that you are defining your brother only as a body. Look closely and you will see the perfection of his spirit underneath."

To put it simply, this world is messed up. If it weren't, we wouldn't be here. We are here on purpose, serving a mission. Our spiritual mission is partly personal—but it is also universal. We are here to learn, but also to share. We are here to help change the world. Nothing—cruelty, abuse, violence, or hatred—can damage our spirits, and it is only through the acquisition of a body that we can make the world a better place. There is healing in the afterlife, but sometimes, there is real hell "here."

John's little girl didn't die in vain. It's sad—and wrong—that she died, but her death invited John to see the reality of the Divine, to embrace the possibility of an afterlife, and to know that love stretches beyond "the veil." She gave, even as she was taken. Can we, too, give no matter what else is happening?

The Plane of Evaluation—for the Living

Ultimately, the goal of all evaluations is to heal shame. Shame is affected by grace—which is the path of the Planes of Light. A short version of the steps along this path includes acknowledgment, compassion and understanding, forgiveness, and change. The outline on the next page offers methods for accomplishing these steps by evaluating our lives as we live them.

- *Confess.* Confession is good for the soul — as long as our aim is to reduce shame, not create more of it. Confession is as easy as talking freely with a friend, working with a good therapist, or writing down your daily dreams, desires, and feelings.

- *Differentiate between judging and discerning.* To judge is to make something or someone "bad." There is no "bad"; there are simply mistakes, which are caused by limited experience or understanding. To discern is to make decisions based on what suits your value system. We can only choose for ourselves, not for others.

- *Live the Native American saying and "walk in another's moccasins."* If you have a problem with someone else, imagine yourself living as they do.

- *Walk in your own moccasins.* Observe the behavior you dislike about yourself and ask what "age" of self is acting that way. We behave like children when we are stuck in a childhood aspect of the self. How would you help a child with this problem? Do the same for yourself.

- *Learn how to forgive; it is a skill.* Study the scriptures that mean something to you, or take a class in forgiveness. Better yet — decide to forgive. It's all about making a decision.

- *Set an "improvement goal."* Shame disintegrates when we change what makes us feel shameful. Every day, select one action that will increase your self-love.

- *Change your mind about the past.* Most of us believe that the past recreates itself. This is not true; nothing ever repeats. We might see reality the same way, and thus respond in the same way, but that does not mean that the same situation has arisen. Everything is always new, and you can decide to become something or someone new, at will.

- *Put on your "God glasses."* What if you could see a situation, yourself, or another person through the eyes of the Divine? This is the ultimate test and experience of higher evaluation, release, and forgiveness.

- *Energetically.* Use red stones or wear red if you want to encourage an evaluative mood. Garnet earrings or pendants will balance the adrenals, and you can discharge negativity into iron to free yourself from old issues. You can also use intention to draw strength from an iron object.

- *Visit the zones.* Work with an energy healer or a spiritual director, or meditate by yourself, and deliberately return to each of the four zones.

In the *white zone,* ask to reconnect with your original guides. Ask to perceive your original soul contract—the decisions you made for the upcoming life and the reasons for them. Check to see if there are any agreements you would now change.

In the *gray zone,* ask the guides to help you access any past or in-between life memories that would serve you today. Ask for spiritual guidance to integrate these memories.

In the *red zone,* feel the emotions you have repressed. Feelings are messengers; each presents a clue or a message for today's life:

- *Happiness:* Keep doing what you are doing.
- *Fear:* Change direction, something is not working.
- *Anger:* You have to establish parameters or boundaries to take better care of yourself.
- *Sadness:* You have lost track of the love in a certain situation, and must search for it.
- *Disgust:* This person or substance is bad for you. Get rid of it.

In the *black zone,* ask to speak to any people or groups that have annoyed, bothered, or plagued you, as well as those you have hurt or injured. How can you repair what has happened? How can you forgive yourself or others for the resulting predicaments? Discover ways to release cords, curses, and other energetic problems, topics I cover in my book *Advanced Chakra Healing.*

CHAPTER 10

THE THIRD PLANE: THE PLANE OF HEALING

CHAKRA Second. Housed in the abdomen region, the second chakra operates our feelings and creativity.

AURA Second auric field, which lies just outside the tenth chakra. This field processes feelings.

CHAKRIC COLOR Orange.

CHAKRIC GLAND Ovaries or testes.

CHAKRIC ELEMENT Cobalt, a transitional metal known for its magnetic (or attractive) qualities and its abilities to transform what is not working into a healthy, operating state.

Overview of the Plane of Healing

To heal means to make whole. On earth, we spend vast amounts of time and money fixing what we think is broken. On the Plane of Healing there are no costs; we have only to recognize our innate wholeness.

We are whole. Whether alive or deceased, in bodily or in soul form, we are always whole, for we are made in the image of the Creator. We might not be as advanced as the Divine, but we are of no less value than it is. Neither are we worth less than anyone or anything else. A three-year-old is not less important or lovable than a thirty-year-old, merely younger and less mature.

We need healing because when we stretch and grow, we fall and get bruised. On the Plane of Healing, we learn how to accept our inner wholeness and align with our spirits. We heal our injuries. Healing is a complex process during life. It is even more so in death; it involves making amends to the living—without being alive ourselves.

Have you ever had a visitation from someone who died? Have you had a dream in which your father or mother said, "I am sorry"? That interaction was conducted through the Plane of Healing: the space that, in seeking forgiveness, grants healing—for the living and the dead.

The Affiliation with the Second Chakra and Auric Field

The second chakra regulates our feelings and creativity. Science is showing that there are nearly as many neurotransmitters regulating emotion in the gut as there are in the brain. The abdomen really is the emotional heart of the body.

From feelings comes creativity. The second chakra acts like a screen, deciding whose feelings can enter our own system and which of our feelings we can share. Soul programming often confuses this process. By the time most of us die, we will have hurt others and ourselves by acting on our feelings, and acquired a basket of feelings that are not our own. But we must be emotionally clean to operate in wholeness. Forgiveness for self and others, as well as from others, are the keys to emotional healing, and therefore the keys to the Plane of Healing.

Cobalt is a crucial energy for transmuting others' feelings into usable material. Scientists are excited about its role in healing cancer and in creating magnetic fields. The lesson of cobalt is that we gain in spiritual energy when we free ourselves from negativity. We can only do this when we are ready to embrace our wholeness and stop making excuses for why we cannot be who and what we really are.

The Wisdom of the Plane of Healing

The wisdom of healing is forgiveness, or pardoning someone for making a mistake. On this Plane, we might need to visit the living to make restitution or help someone who needs it — or spend time forgiving ourselves. Here, to accomplish forgiveness, we might undergo the following process on this Plane:

- Working with the masters to forgive oneself
- Working with the guides of the living — or of other souls that have passed into the afterlife — in order to make amends
- Working with the living to help make their lives better, thereby making whole what was seemingly broken
- Acknowledging oneself as whole

A soul graduates from this Plane when it is able to actively change its erroneous ways while continuing to embrace compassion for self and others.

The Structure of the Plane of Healing

Because of the need for interaction between the living and the nonliving (and sometimes the nonliving with each other), this Plane is highly malleable, with many portals for traveling souls.

The Plane of Healing is an interdimensional crossroads. It is like a town center, with all roads leading to it and away from it. Avenues of the past, present, and future, as well as of life and death, converge at this center point. Here the student soul can connect with all souls from any time period and repair broken relationships.

Some visiting souls reside in the center of this Plane and project their images into other spaces. On earth, we would experience these souls as phantoms, projections of the departed soul, or perhaps interactive dreams. Other souls actually journey from the Plane of Healing to the land of the living, to any time necessary. They can also connect with ghosts on earth or souls on other Planes of Light. A soul can go wherever or whenever it needs in order to make amends and practice a new way of being.

Sometimes a healing soul will visit his or her own past self. Our child selves are frequently stuck in the past, often in abusive situations. What we experience as a guide or angel might be our future (or afterlife) self coming to help us. When we heal the past, we heal the future. Healing souls are often encouraged to return to the four zones to converse with other souls and perform soul repair.

The Masters on the Plane of Healing

There is a nearly infinite number of guides that can attend the healing soul. The most common include:

- Masters of healing.
- Souls of the deceased or the living who have learned what we need to learn: Yes—the living as well as the dead can be guides!
- Healing angels of light: There are angels devoted exclusively to healing, and they are the mainstay on the Plane of Healing. Usually, a single angel of healing is appointed the chief guardian and guide of an entering soul and serves as a companion to the process.

Potential Challenges

Two main problems arise on this Plane:

- We only want to heal others, not ourselves.
- We only want to heal ourselves, not others.

Deceased souls act similarly in death to how they did when alive. It has been said that there are only two kinds of people: givers and takers. Giver souls have a hard time receiving love. They will happily share energy, love, truth, and healing with others, but do not believe they deserve to accept the same. Taker souls are so empty, they cannot imagine actually providing for others; they only want to take. A soul is ready to graduate from this Plane when it can recognize wholeness in itself *and* others in spite of any wounds.

The Plane of Healing — For the Living

There are so many splendid ways to conduct healing while we live—as it is done "in heaven," not "on earth." Here are some steps you can take that encourage wholeness:

- *Make amends.* Twelve-step programs offer brilliant methods for ongoing healing. One of the most vital components is to continually review and forgive, making amends when we are the one creating problems.
- *Change.* We can feel sorry, but a truly sorry person changes his or her own behavior as well.
- *Create an accountability relationship.* By joining a support group, we receive the nonshaming encouragement that we need to become as loving as we are able to. If you are not comfortable with a group or cannot find one, get an accountability friend. Talk every day. At the beginning of the relationship, set goals. In your daily discussion time, review the day before — honestly. Give yourself compliments and analyze what did not work. Then set new goals or focus points for that day (or the next). If possible, refrain from giving feedback. You are self-monitoring, not other-monitoring.
- *Work with a professional.* There are hundreds of different kinds of healers, traditional and alternative. We all need help!
- *Visit the zones.* The zones are great sites for healing. In them, we can receive clear information and interact with souls living and passed. It is often easier and more effective to have a "therapy session" with the soul of a living person in one of the zones than to deal with him or her in everyday life.
- *Energetically.* Use orange stones, clothing, or other orange objects to balance your emotions. Program cobalt jewelry

with positive intention to assist this chakra in accessing the Healing Plane. The easiest way to do this is to hold the jewelry in your hands and either pray into it or ask the Divine's unconditional love to program the metal for you.

- *Pray for those who dwell in the afterlife.* The angels fly the prayers to the appropriate zones and souls. Why not send love on angels' wings?

CHAPTER 11

THE FOURTH PLANE: THE PLANE OF KNOWLEDGE

CHAKRA Third. Located in the solar plexus, this chakra assimilates and organizes information—psychic and mental. Because of this capability, it manages personal power, self-esteem, and self-confidence.

AURA Third auric field, found just outside the second auric layer. It appears as a net that collects and disseminates information.

CHAKRIC COLOR Yellow.

CHAKRIC GLAND The pancreas.

CHAKRIC ELEMENT Copper, which is processed in the digestive system and vital to many neurological functions.

Overview of the Plane of Knowledge

What excites you the most? Shakespeare? Fishing? Studying spiritual matters? We don't lose our interests when we die; on the contrary, our passions intensify because learning accelerates.

On the Plane of Knowledge, souls pursue the subjects that arouse them. Knowledge is the basis of decision making, and here is a Plane entirely devoted to it. Here, soul-scholars might spend years or eons roaming the bookshelves of the universe. Are you interested in horses, butterflies, miniature trains? You can deepen your study of them on the Plane of Knowledge, a matrix of energy that stores all information, known and yet to be discovered. At the same time, the masters of knowledge will challenge you to move beyond the merely personal—or sometimes, even egocentric—interests in certain subjects and stretch into a more universal stratosphere. Can you not only *acquire* knowledge, but also *apply* it? Can you *integrate* varieties of information so as to achieve a higher purpose? Even better, can you *create* new knowledge that brings light where there is darkness?

Many souls begin their work on the Plane of Knowledge feeling ecstatic about pursuing their individual interests; therefore, at one level, this is a "personal" Plane. Personal Planes encourage self-development and assist the soul with penetrating its own psyche. (The other personal Planes include Rest, Evaluation, and Healing.) In order to successfully complete this Plane, however, a soul must graduate to a more universal approach to knowledge. At this point, the Plane provides an impersonal invitation for the soul to evolve. You might say, then, that the Knowledge Plane is the pivot point between exploring yourself and embracing the All.

Affiliation with the Third Chakra and Auric Field

Where else could the Plane of Knowledge connect but at the third chakra, the center of information and organization? The third auric field interfaces with data from everywhere. Its associated organ, the pancreas, is vital for assimilating sweetness into the body;

and the ultimate test of knowledge is how "sweet" or desirable it is. Moreover, copper, which is processed by the digestive system, is necessary for just about any neurological function, including brain function.

The Wisdom Schools on the Plane of Knowledge

There is no end to the breadth and depth of knowledge, and an infinite number of wisdom schools are accessible through the Plane of Knowledge. This Plane is like a huge highway system, with tunnels and portals leading off into different dimensions. Travel one of these and you might find Albert Einstein contemplating the mysteries of the universe. Follow another to acquire sword skills with Joan of Arc. On this Plane, you can pursue what is important to you—and it might take thousands of years.

In some ways, earth is its own Plane of Knowledge. Many esoterics call it a "soul school," and most philosophers are eager to tell us what the lesson plan should be. In actuality, earth is unique in that you write your own lesson plan—and change it if you want. The Plane of Knowledge is the perfect place to fine-tune our earth studies, or to create new paths of learning. To graduate, however, we must eventually leave our solitary library and place what we've learned in context and in relationship. Knowledge alone doesn't provide the perspective we need.

Physics outlines a theory that explains a little about how knowledge works on this Plane. Stick with me—I'm first going to talk about a rather complex theory called the *superposition of waves*, which explains how waves interact. As you read through this theory, think about knowledge as traveling in waves with a single wave representing a certain set of information.

Superposing occurs when two or more similar waves combine to create a third, more complex one. The waves that join form something new—but also keep on going as they were before. Some waves operate a little differently, however. *Interference* occurs when two waves start at the same point but approach each other from different directions. When the two waves are in phase, or in rhythm with each other, the result is a *constructive interference,* or reinforcement. The resulting wave is twice as amplified as the original ones. You get more! *Destructive interference* occurs when the waves are out of synch, and now they cancel each other out. But wait—there's more.

There's also a wave called a *standing* or *stationary wave.* It's a wave that doesn't move. It's formed when two progressive waves come from opposite directions and meet—and then create a harmonically pleasing, vertical wave.

Knowledge works a lot like the mixing and meeting of waves. We want to acquire knowledge—waves of energy—that can merge and form a powerful outcome. We want to "superpose" our areas of learning and get a great result. Think of what might happen if you combined knowledge of chemistry with knowledge of cooking—maybe a terrific chocolate cake. We don't want to mix knowledge areas that cancel each other out, such as putting together information about toxic elements and murder. Ultimately, we want to shape "standing wave forms" or long-lasting testimonies to learning: great thoughts that contribute throughout time, such as Madame Curie's or Sir Isaac Newton's contributions to science. So when you explore the Plane of Knowledge, be aware of how your lines of inquiry combine, and strive to add to the library knowledge that achieves the highest good.

The Masters on the Plane of Knowledge

There are countless knowledge masters on the Plane of Knowledge. Some have been alive; others have not. Each, however, represents the highest ideals of its particular interest area. You might find any of the following types of beings on this Plane:

- *Souls that excelled in their particular knowledge base when alive:* Many of our most intelligent and thoughtful scholars, inventors, and scientists quickly transcend the lower Planes and continue to operate from the Plane of Knowledge. They often inform living people of their new insights, continually sharing their knowledge with the earth. Many also reincarnate at a certain point, so they can directly infuse the world with information. These incoming souls often present as incredibly focused children who know exactly what they want to study, and why.

- *Seraphim:* Seraphim are angels that represent certain kinds of knowledge or principles. One might represent feminine beauty, another impartiality, still another, the honor of the warrior. They often guide souls seeking knowledge into the higher ideals involved in their areas of interest.

- *Muses:* Muses sing with joy whenever a soul pursues a higher understanding of music, literature, or art. Muses seek harmony and support a soul in "attuning" with the entire universe.

- *Forms:* Forms are beings that not only serve truth, but *are* truth. These beings are reminiscent of a story told by the Greek philosopher, Plato. According to Plato, "Forms" (also called virtues) are conscious beings that dwell in a heavenly Cave of Forms. They project their truths downward onto the earth but cannot walk upon it because of its lower vibration. While we are alive, we can glimpse higher truths, but we cannot relate to them. After death, we can actually work with the Forms, who will transmit higher awareness directly into our souls.

- *Masters of knowledge:* There are beings that devote their entire, infinite existence to researching a particular knowledge base. They actually run the different "colleges" of the Plane of Knowledge.

Potential Challenges

It is easy to become so enamored of information that we forget what else is important, such as relationships, or actually applying the data to which we are so devoted. Thus, the challenges of the Plane of Knowledge are many:

- *Pride.* It is easy to think that we are better than others if we think we know more than they do.

- *Temptation.* When you have information about a person, you can be tempted to use it to control him. Some masters of knowledge become swollen with the power inherent in their knowledge. Many return to earth, bodily or as entities, to use knowledge to get what they want. When alive, these souls often rise to prominent positions in their fields, frequently seeking high positions in business or government in order to be in command.

- *Disassociation.* It is easy to lose ourselves in knowledge to prevent potentially painful interaction. A dusty book can seem preferable to the prospect of a critical tongue.

- *Lower versus higher learning.* Facts by themselves might be true, but not necessarily truthful. For example, my son shared a silly story with me. "Mom," he said, "did you know that everyone who has ever eaten bread is going to die?" It is true, isn't it? Everyone who has eaten bread—or drunk water or slept in a bed or kissed a spouse—is going to die. There is no causal relationship, however. A true master of knowledge doesn't use facts to deceive.

The Plane of Knowledge — For the Living

You may already be living on the Plane of Knowledge, or have returned from there in order to continue both the research and application of knowledge. Are you in love with a certain subject area? Devoted to the pursuit of higher knowledge? Are you ever-curious and eager to learn and share your passion? Then you are already either entranced with the Plane of Knowledge, an enrolled student in one of its schools, or maybe even a graduate!

Here are some tips for affirming and evolving knowledge during your lifetime:

- *Pursue your passions.* Knowledge ignites the soul, calling it more fully into the body.
- *Get a mentor.* There are mentors among the living and those existing in soul form, and you need both. Join a group, hire a consultant, read books, follow the living leaders in your chosen field of study. And remember, you can also ask for an adviser from the afterlife when in meditation, or pray for the aid of a master spiritual teacher from the Plane of Knowledge. Evaluate teachers, living or not, by whether they have maintained integrity in all they have done. It's important to select people who have embraced the everyday life, rather than hoarding knowledge or avoiding reality.
- *Seek to contribute, not inhibit.* Don't withhold or attempt to control the dissemination of what you've learned. Know also that the ends never justify unethical means; the path of achievement must be as life- and love-affirming as the final product. We must question the medical achievements of Adolf Hitler, for instance, who used horrific means to acquire knowledge during World War II, employing scientists to experiment on children and other innocents. Some of his results have helped people since—but the process was not ethical.

A true master of knowledge doesn't hurt others to acquire information.

•. *Energetically.* Have yellow stones or objects nearby while you learn. Discharge mental "programs" that keep you from learning and those that encourage the acquisition of misinformation into citrine, sulfur rocks, or copper bracelets. Consider programming a copper bracelet to boost the association between your third chakra and the Plane of Knowledge. You can also imagine a bright copper light and energetically insert it into your third chakra to enhance an appropriate relationship with knowledge.

• *Be a mentor.* When we teach, we learn. There are numerous mentoring programs and opportunities to guide others.

CHAPTER 12

THE FIFTH PLANE: THE PLANE OF WISDOM

CHAKRA Fourth. The "heart chakra" is physically located within the heart, the center of love and relationships.

AURA Fourth auric field, which covers the third auric field.

CHAKRIC COLOR Green.

CHAKRIC GLAND The heart.

CHAKRIC ELEMENT Palladium, known as a metal of wisdom.

Overview of the Plane of Wisdom

Wisdom is a pivotal Plane. Here, souls begin gaining momentum after integrating knowledge with experience: this is the definition of wisdom.

At lower Planes, learning was either personal or factual. Wisdom merges personal experiences, which have been processed in the first three Planes, with the higher teachings of the fourth-Plane knowledge, to open the windows of the soul for enlightenment.

A story about King Solomon of ancient times reveals the importance of wisdom. God asked Solomon what he desired: earthly goods, women, power, or fame. Solomon considered his choices, and gave a surprise answer: wisdom. God was so happy with Solomon's thinking that he gave him wisdom *and* everything else!

Affiliation with the Fourth Chakra and Auric Field

The heart is the center of both the spiritual and physical bodies. It emits five thousand times more electricity than does the brain, and is now known as a major endocrine gland, manufacturing hormones that affect love, behavior, and health. The fourth auric field interconnects us relationally with the living and the dead—as well as with all aspects of ourselves. It is said that we are creatures of relationship. The truth is that the entire universe is about relationship.

Palladium is named after Pallas Athena, the goddess of wisdom and love. It makes sense that this metal—as well as the heart—would serve as the point for attaining wisdom. What good are experience and knowledge without the perspective of love?

Cultivating Wisdom: The Ultimate Goal

The goal of wisdom is enlightenment. Enlightenment is a common theme among spiritual seekers.

The word *enlightenment* actually means "in light" or "with the light." As we have explored, we are made of light, as is everything. True wisdom begins with seeing the light in darkness, the good beneath the bad, hope within despair. Students on the Plane of Wisdom graduate when they are able to make decisions that enlighten themselves and others. These decisions meet the following characteristics:

- *Balance.* A wise soul understands that knowledge and experience are equally important. Think—and do. Do—then think. And learn from what you have done or thought.
- *Acceptance.* Wisdom is contingent on accepting the past. A wise person keeps the past in the past, accepts what has been learned, and keeps moving forward.
- *Paring down knowledge.* Concern yourself with quality, not quantity. It's not how much you know, it's how useful that knowledge is.
- *Willingness to share, with respect.* It is important for us to learn our own lessons, but the true merit of a master lies in the desire to give to others. Even here, the key is balance. You can teach and show others the way, but you also have to allow them to create their own paths—and make their own mistakes.
- *Knowing which side to choose.* There are two sides to every coin. You can use your wisdom to wage war—or to make peace.
- *Readiness to see truth, not just wisdom.* Wisdom can bend with personal experience; truth will not. Truth will accommodate everyone's needs, not only one's own. This is the basis for going to the next level.

The Process of the Plane of Wisdom

The Plane of Wisdom is less defined, less tangible, than any of the previous Planes. The best analogy is a kaleidoscope of various hues of colors.

These colors are actually made of the superpositioned standing wave forms that were described in the previous chapter. Wisdom is like a chef, mixing and stirring knowledge with experience, creating blends that support our higher spiritual purpose.

Masters on the Plane of Wisdom

There are three qualifications for a master on the Plane of Wisdom:

- Life experience
- Special knowledge
- A desire to help others develop wisdom

The types of beings usually found on this Plane are:

- *The Wise Ones:* Ours is not the first universe. Many traditions, including Vedic, Hopi, and Mayan, speak of earlier creations. Some big-bang theorists hypothesize that this universe started from a spark created when an earlier universe collapsed. Souls from other universes often converge on the Planes of Light to help struggling souls; the Wise Ones are beings from other universes who are helping this one. Many of the Wise Ones were incarnated in earlier ages on earth. Our race seems to be a declining one, continually descending in both light and ability. The Wise Ones reappear to help us reevolve. They constitute the primary guides on the Plane of Wisdom.

- *Avatars:* These souls, when incarnate, ascended without physically dying. Ascension involves quickening the body's frequency so that it matches the soul's higher vibrations. Among spiritual beings, avatars are uniquely capable of understanding a human soul's needs, as they are still human themselves.

- *The dream self:* This aspect of self often awakens on the Plane of Wisdom. The ancestral wisdom of some cultures, such as the Hawaiian kahuna, relates that all of life is a dream: we spin reality from the dreams of the "dream self." This self is suspended within the soul. When we are alive, we usually hold it away from our bodies, thus limiting its contact and effectiveness. This separation also creates an artificial environment for the dream self. Disconnected from the heart, it dreams disasters more often than desires. On the Plane of Wisdom, the dream self is encouraged to fully awaken and become conscious of what it is manifesting and why. When the dream self is animate, it feels and experiences, and its decisions will be made with compassion and care.

Potential Challenges

Some of the challenges to face on the Plane of Wisdom are:

- *Pride.* Is a "wise soul" really wise—or does it just think it is? Truly smart people do not think of themselves as smart; instead, they are curious.

- *Misinterpretation of experience.* Some souls judge experience as more valuable than knowledge. This can lead to faulty decision making.
- *Overemphasis on knowledge.* Knowledge alone only takes you so far. Some souls find solace—and a hiding place—in knowledge, preferring to forget about experience.
- *Seriousness.* Many so-called "wise" people take everything, including themselves, too seriously. This is not wisdom; it is self-consciousness.

The Plane of Wisdom — For the Living

Here are the secrets of wisdom for those who seek it while alive:

- *Do not take your life experiences personally.* You have amassed quite a collection of memories and scars. Do you really think that everyone who caused you pain wanted to hurt you? You cannot become wise until you stop thinking that it's all about you.
- *Activate your intuition.* Before you act or speak, stop and think—and access your intuition. Intuition gets us out of the box of prior experience and reveals more enlightened ways to respond.
- *Get out of the past.* Most people believe that they are responding to events in the present, when they are simply triggering memories of yesterday. Use some of the more advanced techniques available from therapists, including regression processes, to unhook from the

past. I recommend Eye Movement Desensitization and Reprocessing (EMDR), administered by a professional psychologist, or Voice Stress Analysis, a computer-based system that releases subconscious memories.

- *Empower yourself across time.* To a certain degree, we have control of both the future and the past. With a change of perspective, you can alter the effects of the past. By setting goals, you can forge a better future.

- *Energetically.* Use stones such as emerald, fluorite, and jade to energetically boost the heart's spiritual and physical functioning. Draw upon the energy of palladium—perhaps even thinking of the Divine feminine energy of Pallas Athena—to encourage the correct spin of this chakra.

- *Develop and practice a sense of humor.* There is nothing more important than enjoying life. The truly wise don't forget this; they live in a state of delight.

CHAPTER 13

THE SIXTH PLANE: THE PLANE OF TRUTH

CHAKRA Fifth. Housed in the throat, this is the center of communication.

AURA Fifth auric field, found outside of the fourth auric field and connected to celestial realms.

CHAKRIC COLOR Blue.

CHAKRIC GLAND The thyroid.

CHAKRIC ELEMENT Quicksilver (mercury), named after Hermes, the messenger god.

Overview of the Plane of Truth

The world is established on spiritual truths, such as faith, hope, justice, and clarity. These are the fundamental energies of the universe and of what is called our *spiritual DNA,* the energies that reflect our true essence and can be activated by the light. All truths support unconditional love.

A soul ascends to the Plane of Truth when it is ready to release its personal issues and theories of reality and to actually *become* truth. Our spirit carries universal truths, but the Plane of Truth helps our souls *transform into* universal truths.

Affiliation with the Fifth Chakra and Auric Field

Many people say that truth depends on your perspective. Through the Plane of Truth, we elevate our particular individual perspective to the mountaintop — the viewpoint of our Divine self. Here, we access the universal truths that enable the climb to consciousness.

The back side of the fifth chakra receives this higher guidance. Through the front side, we share these messages with the world. Some of what comes in is helpful and some is harmful — as is what goes out. Many life — and afterlife — lessons are devoted to figuring out how to receive and send information so that it meets higher goals. And what physical element is more appropriate to this task than mercury, another term for the messenger god Hermes?

The Structure of the Plane of Truth

When we are alive, we think about truth, but often consider that truths are just thoughts. They are much more; they are tangible energies. Spiritual truths are actually made of the superpositioned standing wave forms that we discussed in the last two chapters. These interconnect to form matrixes or grids. Masters of truth are able to perceive these truths in their real form and also merge them. And they can distinguish between the two fundamental matrixes, or grids, of truth.

The Secondary Grid regulates our human existence and continues to enfold souls in the afterlife. This grid is chiefly composed of the dysfunctional beliefs, lies, and falsities that run our world. The individual standing wave forms might be "true," but they aren't put together in a healthy way. For instance, this grid might interconnect ideas like "love" and "religion" to reach a principle such as "God loves you if you're religious." Beliefs like this have caused the deaths of millions of people over time at the hands of "do-gooders" who believe that it's their right to enforce this "spiritual" maxim.

The Star Grid, or Primary Grid, comprises "true truths." These truths are made up of spiritual values that, when conjoined, create positive outcomes. For instance, "religion" might be fastened together with "joy," thus defining religion as a path that produces joy.

When we are alive, our physical genes interlace with the Secondary Grid. Many problems and diseases are carried on these physical genes. Our spiritual genetics, however, can countermand physical genetics, bolstering healing and supporting our general well-being. These genes connect to the Primary Grid, but are only effective when activated. Accessing the Planes during life encourages the shifts that awaken these genetics.

Masters on the Plane of Truth

Following are the masters most typically found on the Plane of Truth. Several of these masters, including the Ancient Ones and the Seraphim, work with all students of truth.

- *The Ancient Ones:* The Ancient Ones were present at the inception of the universe and follow the first laws of creation, which are called the Ancient Laws. These are practical laws that attune to truth, and all students of truth must learn how to use them. They include:

  Law of the innocent. No one has the right to hurt, lie to, or injure the innocent. Innocents are assured angelic protection and support, until they reach a state or age of development that invites free will.

  Law of abundance. Everything and everyone in the universe is entitled to have their basic needs met.

  Law of clarity. A being of any nature must reveal its true nature, if asked.

- *Seraphim:* Each student of truth works with at least one Seraphim, an angelic being that represents a higher ideal such as being merciful or taking care of the needy.

- *Archangels:* Archangels oversee particular concerns. Michael, for instance, fights evil, while Gabriel serves as a messenger. Archangels often teach with one another, together showing a soul how to implement ideals for positive results.

- *Archons:* These are guides that oversee rules and judgments. They lead classes in the appropriate use of authority.

- *Prophets and seers: Prophets* are beings that reveal destinies—universal, group, or personal. *Seers* foresee the future. Students of truth must develop their own expertise in these matters to whatever level is possible so that they can track the Divine's wishes for self and other (prophecy) and make wise decisions based on possible outcomes (precognition).

Potential Challenges

What can derail a potential master of truth? Lies—and truth.

It can be hard to be honest with ourselves. We want to see ourselves in the best light, but sometimes we don't like what we see. It's also true that some of us don't want to see ourselves in a good light! On the Plane of Truth, we must address the following six basic lies in order to perceive ourselves truthfully:

- I am worthless.
- I am bad.
- I have no value.
- I do not deserve.
- I am powerless.
- I am unlovable.

No one—whether alive or dwelling in the afterlife—can defeat these lies by asserting their opposites. You can argue a sense of worthlessness by deciding that you are worthy, but contrary beliefs always indicate captivity on the Secondary Grid. A master of truth either calls upon an Ancient Law to promote healing or creates a higher principle to obtain a Divine perspective. For instance, instead of believing oneself worthy or not worthy, why not promote the value of authenticity?

Unfortunately, some souls do not overcome the six lies. They do not accept their own inherent purity. Some of these will return to earth as egomaniacs, using "truths" from the Secondary Grid to manipulate others to achieve authority. Others will incarnate and develop severe schizophrenia, manic depression, paranoia, suicidal tendencies, or addictions to hide from their "badness." Others remain in soul form and attach to the living, fueling their lies to gain a sense of power.

The Plane of Truth — For the Living

Here are some ideas for living in truth:

- *Read ancient scriptures.* Most scripture emphasizes truth. Do not read the laws — read through them into the *meaning,* which will always emphasize love.
- *Listen beneath the words.* Draw upon your intuition to assess what is genuine.
- *Live through your heart.* Only your heart can recognize who and what you really are. Begin every day by taking a few deep breaths and imagining a golden light streaming through your heart, back to front. This is the truth of the Divine. It will support and sustain you throughout the day, providing clarification and instruction as you go.
- *Draw upon the Ancient Laws.* Pretend that you yourself are the Divine, creating the universe. What three or four principles would you put in place to help all beings and creatures? Call upon these ideas on a daily basis.

- *See truth as a living consciousness.* Imagine that the spiritual truths are not only beams of energy, but are maintained by conscious beings. Talk to these beings when you are in need. Have a cup of tea with Faith. Get on the phone with Wisdom.

- *Understand the levels of truth.* Being truthful is not about always being fully honest. You might tell a friend that her outfit looks horrible; that is being honest. But is it the truth? What if her clothing makes her feel beautiful? That is also true. Is the sense of the matter more truthful or solid than the appearance of it?

- *Energetically.* Blue stones, including lapis and blue topaz, can help clear and strengthen the fifth chakra. Of course, you cannot imbibe mercury; instead, ask the assistance of quicksilver to increase this chakra's functionality through visualization while meditating. You can picture the bright silver drops you have seen in a thermometer slowly dripping into your thyroid or fifth chakra as if you were being fed intravenously. If you're seeking protection, imagine spreading a silver lotion on your body.

CHAPTER 14

THE SEVENTH PLANE: THE PLANE OF PEACE

CHAKRA Sixth. Located at the "third eye," or the middle of the forehead. Manages vision, seeing into the future, and self-image.

AURA Sixth auric layer, just outside of the fifth layer. Gathers possibilities and focuses them for manifesting.

CHAKRIC COLOR Purple.

CHAKRIC GLAND Pituitary gland.

CHAKRIC ELEMENT Iridium, which actualizes the dream state, provides healing and higher consciousness, and assists in levitation.

Overview of the Plane of Peace

We all long for peace. We want to watch the news and see people smiling, not suffering from loss of limb or loss of innocence. We want to travel and not have to check terrorism reports. The world as it is can make us cringe.

Having developed the ability to perceive and live in truth, an ascending soul longs to use its knowledge to help others. The key to achieving peace is in understanding that it must be achieved internally before it can be created externally. When you are complete inside, you can help make the world whole. Thus, the key word for the student of peace is *integrity.*

Affiliation with the Sixth Chakra and Auric Field

Whether consciously or not, you rely upon your sense of *clairvoyance,* or inner sight, to assess your needs and manifest your desires. This ability is housed in your sixth chakra, which is centered in the pituitary. The surrounding sixth auric field catches the dreams of the Divine at the back of the sixth chakra and spins them into the chakra. Through factors including self-image, karmic issues, and dharmic understandings, you select a future and spin it through the front side of the sixth chakra. It is then caught in the net of the chakra and manifested as concrete reality. When activated, the element iridium ensures that your selections suit you and are enjoyable.

We create what we perceive to be true. Do you think that peace is possible? Have you completed the tasks of the personal Planes of Light—the first three Planes—to make peace with yourself? Many students of peace revisit the lower Planes to attain "clear vision." We must be at peace with our past to create a peaceful future. We must have integrity with our personal process before we can serve a higher purpose for others.

The Wisdom of Integrity

Integrity has many meanings. All apply to the peace trainee:

- High moral standards

- Existing in a state of wholeness
- The knowledge of being sound, or undamaged

We don't have to act perfectly in order to have high moral standards, we just need to be who we really are. We can be confused and make mistakes and still have integrity and be whole, simply through accepting ourselves and reaching for higher principles. We don't have to be completely healed or always loving in order to be sound and undamaged; we need only acknowledge that everything we have done—and are doing—can be transformed into goodness. These are the ultimate lessons of the Plane of Peace.

But how do we learn them?

Every student of peace is assigned a master of peace who shadows the student. The master impartially observes everything the student says, does, thinks, and does not do. The master of peace doesn't tell his or her apprentice what to do. Remember our laws of physics? The observer affects the experiment. By being watched, the peaceful student learns how to watch the self.

At some point in their training, most students of peace become teachers. They might assist on one of the other Planes, become a spiritual guide for an earth being, or even reincarnate. Many of today's children are entering from this Plane—the earth is in trouble, and peace masters are coming to help.

Masters on the Plane of Peace

A student of peace will receive one-on-one instruction from at least one of these guides:

- *A Watcher (described in the Special Section and again in chapter 19):* Watchers comprise a group of beings that invite love through observation. Special Watchers dwell on the Plane of Peace to assist in the development of peace everywhere. Some have particular specialties in accordance with their studies on the Plane of Knowledge. Some Watchers might be interested in literature and monitor the activities of authors, those living and those in soul form. Others might excel at negotiating and will scrutinize those who are involved in law or mediation.

- *A former warrior:* Who better to instruct on the topic of peace than a Genghis Khan, Cleopatra, or Alexander the Great—those who have learned from warring and now strive toward peace?

- *Archangels—Powers and Shining Ones: Powers* spin earth energy into the Planes of Light. *The Shining Ones* shift heavenly energies onto the earth. Powers often work with people or souls that have committed (or are committing) evil, to transmute good from bad. Shining Ones carry the truths and energies of the higher realms to earth.

- *Gurus and saints:* These constitute souls who, when alive, served peace. Many were martyred for their efforts. Some rise immediately to a higher Plane, often the Plane of Peace, where they teach the meaning and wisdom of peace.

Potential Challenges

The greatest challenge of peacefulness is complacency. It is easy to confuse peace with serenity, and believe that it is always better to walk away from a fight than participate in it. Sometimes we must assert ourselves for the cause of justice.

The Plane of Peace — For the Living

How do you achieve peace during this lifetime? What a great goal!

- *Ask for transmissions.* Most gurus and higher entities teach through transmission, the psychic conveyance of truth and knowledge through energetic means. Ask the Divine for a master of peace and begin to work with your assigned guide.
- *Accept your current state or condition.* Then change it. Slowly.
- *Use symbols.* Symbology — the use of sacred shapes, sounds, tones, colors, and other representations — calls higher energies into physical form. There are books, including my *Advanced Chakra Healing,* that offer the meanings of a variety of symbols. Learn the language of symbols and begin to use them to further your higher intentions and goals. If you are an erratic and frantic person, for instance, working with squares or rectangles will ground you and help you become more practical. Visualize squares, wear them in accessory form, or even paint them on your walls!
- *Review your feelings.* Feelings lead to peace, but they do not always seem to. All feelings share messages. Assess your feelings daily — even hourly — to see what you are

telling yourself. These messages are described in chapter 9 on the Plane of Evaluation.

- *If you unearth old issues that are causing internal chaos, return to the paths of the three lower Planes.*
- *Energetically.* Stimulate self-love with purple stones or through meditating on the color purple. Iridium is a rare element; concentrate on its energy when praying or meditating to transform the sixth chakra. Iridium can be pictured as a hard, silvery-white substance with a slightly yellow hue. You might want to imagine a medallion of iridium, a hard, brittle object that, when held to your third eye, casts a silver-yellow energy into that chakra.

CHAPTER 15

THE EIGHTH PLANE: THE PLANE OF MOMENTUM

CHAKRA Seventh, located at the top of the head. Center of spirituality and our spiritual destiny.

AURA Seventh auric field, external to the sixth auric field.

CHAKRIC COLOR White.

CHAKRIC GLAND Pineal gland.

CHAKRIC ELEMENT High-spin gold, which activates the pineal gland, creating White Light for the entire body.

Overview of the Plane of Momentum

Imagine that you have spent years — maybe eons — in the land of peace. You have learned self-control. When you are hurt, you do not blame others — but you do take care of yourself emotionally and psychologically. If you make a mistake, you do not shame yourself; you forgive, learn, and move on. You accept yourself, even while you continue to improve in both attitude and deed. Now it is time to extend this internal integrity to others, employing your many resources in achieving your personal destiny.

Destiny isn't something that happens to you; you must act. For example, you must put peace into action if you want to create a world of peace. What is your purpose, your destiny? Infusing it with momentum is like putting wheels on the body of a car. Now, you can *move!*

Affiliation with the Seventh Chakra and Auric Field

The seventh chakra has long been exalted among spiritual enthusiasts. With its basis in the pineal gland, the seventh chakra is the focus of prayer, meditation, and contemplation. It's also the source of prophetic wisdom—the revelations that lead to goodness within and for the world. The seventh auric field interconnects with all spiritual realms— including the Divine—like a ladder to heaven. The ancients have long known that when it is illuminated by high-spin gold, the pineal gland opens like a doorway to the White Light. This energy now stirs the devotee to action.

In their longing for connection to the Divine, many spiritually oriented people forget the essential element of action. But you cannot achieve higher goals without movement. Scriptures from every culture and race emphasize the heroism of prophets, seers, and gurus. Just the same, some kinds of actions won't get us very far. We don't want to end up like poor Jonah, who in fleeing God's commands ended up in the belly of a whale. Thus, one of the challenges of the Plane of Momentum is to make sure that our movement is getting us someplace we want to go.

The Wisdom of the Plane of Momentum

On the Plane of Momentum, we are called to conduct ourselves with *scrutinized action,* behaving only under and through Divine orders. A momentum soul is therefore assigned one or many acts of service, which are overseen by a master. The tasks might include:

- Becoming a guide for a living person or a group of living people.
- Becoming a force for nature, serving the earth so as to experience that aspect of the soul.
- Teaching souls that exist on one of the lower Planes of Light.
- Assisting the living with a certain form of expertise.
- Performing a certain "quest," either bodily or in soul form.
- Instructing angels about human nature.
- Working interdimensionally, universally, or in the nonmaterial planes to create change for higher good.
- Preparing other souls to return to life. There are many advanced souls being born on this planet. See the following sidebar to discover which type you are!

A momentum soul-in-training will continue service until it is ready to transcend to the next Plane.

SPECIAL SOULS: WHO'S ON THIS PLANET RIGHT NOW?

Souls tend to incarnate in groups. Our planet is evolving, just as we are as individuals. Following are the main soul groups currently invested in helping this planet progress. They are listed from oldest to youngest.

- *Construct souls:* This, the "grandparent generation," is represented by souls that hold very specific ideas or goals. They were born into a world that required explicit knowledge and expertise, as well as strong values. These people needed to become carpenters or mothers, or to follow the Catholic or Islamic faith, for instance. Many of these souls are working on the Plane of Knowledge or its equivalent on earth.

- *Bridge souls:* The "baby boomer" generation bridges the old with the new, the material with the spiritual. Many returned from the Planes of Evaluation or Healing, knowing that integrity of action calls for personal change first, planetary contributions second. Over the last decades, this understanding stimulated a groundswell in personal growth, from addiction treatment to therapy to "New Age" healing. The challenge for this group is to continue advancing in the higher Planes while devoting the self to personal healing.

- *Indigo souls:* This "twenty-something" generation, which spills down into the teens and up into the thirties, is wisdom-based. They want experience and freedom, but must also accept the responsibilities of developing knowledge to make practical contributions to the planet. Their representative color — indigo — combines blue and purple, the colors of communication and vision. Their ultimate objectives are to establish higher goals for this world and decide how those can be achieved. They can best serve by adhering to the ideas of the Plane of Momentum.

- *Crystal souls:* Crystal souls nearly always come from the higher Planes. They have usually transcended all the lower Planes and represent at least the Plane of Peace and upward. They tend to carry very little karma—or self-protection. Being quite psychic, their challenge is to live in a depressed world and keep themselves free of the negativity present.

- *Spirit souls:* Some souls are incarnating angels, or souls from the very highest Planes. These do not have the protection issues of the crystal children, because they understand compassion and forgiveness and do not perceive danger where there is none. These souls hold the energies of what is possible for this world.

Masters on the Plane of Momentum

Here are the most typical guides on the Plane of Momentum:

- The Forms, or incarnations of higher virtues and ideals.
- Archangels that are service oriented.
- Masters of the higher Planes, especially those from the Plane of Love.
- Muses, distinguished in their artistic areas.

- Former traumatized souls who have worked through their issues and can now help others.
- Seraphim, which represent certain truths.
- Nature spirits, if their presence serves the student's progress. For instance, an air elemental can provide instruction on movement, while a fire elemental can instruct on transmutation.

Sometimes a student of momentum learns by becoming master to a master, or in other words, reversing roles. The goal is to learn scrutiny by scrutinizing another. In these cases, the momentum trainee is usually guided by a master from the Plane of Love who assists the momentum student.

Potential Challenges

Being busy does not necessarily produce accomplishment. Think about cleaning the house. You can move things around but never get the house picked up! Kids are famous for this; what first lies on the floor often ends up under the bed. The greatest danger of momentum is that our actions do not take us anywhere.

There are many reasons we fail to be productive, in life and in soul form. These include:

- *Fear.* We do not really believe that we can accomplish our goal, so we sabotage ourselves. That way we cannot really "fail."
- *False aims.* We are not clear of our end goals; we flail around.

- *Lack of precision.* For actions to be productive, they must be targeted and deliberate.
- *Comparison issues.* Even after death, a soul compares itself to others. Maybe someone else is capable of performing ten acts of grace a day—but our aim is five. Does this make us less important or industrious than the busier soul? No; each path is unique.

The Plane of Momentum — For the Living

If you feel compelled to serve, you're probably at least touching on the Plane of Momentum. This urge is not to be confused with *caretaking,* which involves taking care of others at one's own expense. If you believe that you are ready to gain momentum spiritually, here are a few ways to go about it:

- *Volunteer.* What special gifts do you have? What population or type of person can benefit the most from them? Follow that special tug on your heart.
- *Say "yes" when you can help.* When we're true to our purpose, our everyday lives present us with opportunities to serve. You don't have to travel to Timbuktu or join the Peace Corps to be of service. We are agents of love and peace right where we are.
- *Discover your special abilities.* What is unique about you? What is your higher purpose? There are specific gifts associated with each chakra. They are briefly described in chapter 17 about the Plane of Power.

- *Energetically.* Use quartz or a white stone as an energetic focus when praying or meditating. There are Web sites for procuring high-spin gold homeopathic remedies; I think those developed by David Hudson are the most credible. Consult a healing professional before using any alternative products.

CHAPTER 16

THE NINTH PLANE: THE PLANE OF LOVE

CHAKRA Eighth, located just atop the head. Appearing as a small black dot, this chakra regulates karma and our shamanic powers.

AURA Eighth auric field, just outside of the seventh auric field.

CHAKRIC COLOR Black in the immature, silver in the master.

CHAKRIC GLAND Thymus.

CHAKRIC ELEMENT Silver, for its role in conductivity, boosting the immune system, and psychic activity.

Overview of the Plane of Love

Love is a paradox. It is everything—but it's also what it isn't!

How can love be hatred, cruelty, and greed? On the Plane of Love, you get to ask these questions—and hopefully, come up with acceptable answers. Love is certainly a thorny bush, and figuring it out is the job of the eighth chakra shaman.

Affiliation with the Eighth Chakra and Auric Field

The eighth chakra is the world of the shaman. At some level, we are all shamans, able to connect all worlds and travel the dimensions with speed and alacrity. Many of us stifle these powers, however, because they can be confounding and confusing. Shamans, you see, do everything in reverse. If you tell a shaman to create peace, he will first make war. If you ask a shaman to move aside, she might first come closer to you. Such is the way of shaman—and of the Divine.

We don't often recognize the presence of love on this planet—or in our lives—because we think conditionally. What better place to learn about love—unconditional love—than in the shadowy realm of the shaman, where you can only understand an issue by examining it from both sides, not just one? Silver is the ideal metal for this activity, as it has been associated historically with the perception of truth and the deflection of lies.

Mirrors are key tools in the shamanic realm. They are painted silver, and it's interesting that they provide reverse, rather than direct, images. On the Plane of Love, we often have to look at what something isn't to see what it is.

The Wisdom of Being Love (Or, If We're Made of Love . . . Why Isn't the World More Loving?)

There is one way to operate on or graduate from the Plane of Love. It is to accept yourself—and everything else—as being made of love.

When we look around the world, it is hard to imagine that the fundamental unit of matter is love. It is equally challenging to consider what sort of Creator would form a world like this one. Regardless of the Creator's original intent, if God were really loving, why wouldn't he—or she—step in and clean up this mess?

The Plane of Love makes us face these issues, which leads us to two conclusions. First, the world and our lives and our souls are a mess because love cannot impose conditions; if it did, it would not be love. Before separating from Source, we floated in an idyllic sea. We thought it would be wonderful to descend to the river of death and life, and share our spiritual truths with others. Must love look a certain way? Is it love to force someone else to be kind? Is it love to hate ourselves because we do not look, act, or think "perfectly"?

If we are made of love, we are capable of being loving. To achieve this lofty goal in a physical or soul state, however, we must be given the power to not be loving. We must be shamans, beings who mediate all sides of reality and then choose what is loving—not by appearance, but by sensing it.

Your shaman self, which is highlighted on the Plane of Love, is able to see through the sham of false love and make truly loving decisions. The master of love—the shaman of love—can embrace all that the Creator has created because he or she has realized a very important fact:

We *are* the Creator.

If we were present in the Source—in God, the Great Luminary, the Almighty—before time, then we are part of the environment that formed the rules of manifestation. We formulated a world of pain and suffering because we required that environment to learn about unconditionality. In our deliberate and awesome wisdom, we placed conditions on love so that we could defy them.

Of course, the soul devolution process caused us to forget this salient fact. We have forgotten the usefulness of free will. You give money to someone who is impoverished, and he steals from you. You give your heart to a lover, and she rips it in shreds before flinging it back in your face. The master of love would laugh and say, "Wow, they are playing the game of love! I think I will go out and love some more." Instead, we establish more conditions on love, and end up being mean and nasty ourselves!

On the Plane of Love, the masters provide us with tasks to make us stop waiting for perfection before we are willing to be loving. What are these tasks? They will, of necessity, involve dealing with our own or others' imperfections. They might take us to "hell." They might invite us to "walk in" to the body of a prison inmate, or to incarnate into a Mafia family. Whatever the cost, the lesson is worth the price.

Masters on the Plane of Love

The Plane of Love is a somber yet inspiring place. No soul passes into the "thirteenth Plane," the state of knowing, without first serving as a master on this Plane. There are no specific types of masters here; the only qualification is that the master must be completely loving toward the student.

This is not always so easy to do—or to take. Imagine that your parents had loved you unconditionally. Do you think that they would have allowed you to eat cookies all night long? Drink and drive? Masters of love understand the importance of boundaries. Even more essential, a master of love knows that the student must figure out his or her own boundaries, which can only be learned through the consequences of action. Real love can be hard to give or receive.

Potential Challenges

The greatest challenge to love is figuring out the relationship between acceptance and boundaries. On one hand, an unconditionally loving person accepts any and everything about him- or herself, others, and the world. Love and judgment don't correlate.

Or do they?

What if someone hits you? What if someone strikes your child? Would you allow violence? It's easy to err on the side of being too accepting—and therefore, a weakling, effective at nothing and good for no one. It's also tempting to establish boundaries that are too rigid, coldheartedly punishing those who don't live up to the highest standards of love. Masters of love trust in the power and wisdom of their hearts, the focal point of true love.

The Plane of Love — For the Living

How do you develop a truly loving nature while you live? Most religions and spiritual disciplines devote themselves to this question. Here are a few ideas that might accelerate your own growth:

- *Think about this question: What if you were made of love?* Honestly, what if every part of you were actually made of Divine material? How would you treat yourself?

How would you act toward others? What would you eat? When would you sleep? What goals would you set—what rules would you break?

- *Heal your heart.* Upon rising, talk to your heart. Ask it to tell or show you how to love yourself as the day goes on. Love is an inside-to-outside job. You will be more able to express love to others if you can first give it to yourself.

- *Heal others' hearts.* What we give away often comes back to us. Every day, create or take advantage of at least one opportunity to show someone else that he or she deserves love.

- *Concentrate on the void.* The Plane of Love is represented as a void, an empty space. It mirrors our own thoughts and perceptions back to us. For a day, decide that the world is mirroring teachings about love. If others are constantly angry with you, ask yourself if they are "mirroring" inappropriate anger you must deal with— or if they are inviting you to get appropriately angry! Always look at two sides of the coin to discover the message being provided.

- *Reframe love.* Imagine that the Divine has turned your heart upside down and inside out so that you can't make any assumptions about love. How can you transform greed, envy, or cruelty into love? How can you see others who come from these spaces with love? Would you put up boundaries? Would you move into acceptance? How do you know what to do?

- *Live in the empty spaces.* Another way to reflect on love is to live in the moments in-between. For every breath we take, there is a flicker of no-breath. Our heart pauses just as often as it beats. We can become anything we want within these empty spaces. Use them to assess situations and make decisions.

- *Establish boundaries.* Our "yes" doesn't mean anything unless we can also say "no." See if you can mean what you say, and say what you mean.

- *Say "thank you" to your adversaries.* Shamans are grateful for their enemies. Even the vilest character teaches us. A cruel boss challenges us to establish boundaries — or maybe look for a new job. A grumpy kid invites patience. If we're trying to develop love, the Divine isn't going to give us loving circumstances, but rather, situations that will call forth love.

- *Energetically.* Focus on your thymus gland, the immune center in your upper chest. In *Vibrational Medicine,* Dr. Richard Gerber provides inspirational ways to connect by communicating with heart-based emotions. Think about how to express love in real ways. Use black stones, such as onyx or obsidian, to absorb your own negativity, and wear silver jewelry to deflect others' harmful energies and to accept divine transmissions. Consider seeing a qualified professional for homeopathic remedies to boost this gland, if needed.

CHAPTER 17

THE TENTH PLANE: THE PLANE OF POWER

CHAKRA Ninth, located an arm's length above the head. Harmonizes our soul with others' souls.

AURA Ninth auric field, right outside the eighth auric layer.

CHAKRIC COLOR Gold.

CHAKRIC GLAND Diaphragm.

CHAKRIC ELEMENT Rhodium, for its role in hardening platinum and its help in achieving higher dream states.

Overview of the Plane of Power

Power is the ability to generate change.

We are all powerful beings because we can influence energy, both inside and outside of ourselves. Most of the time, we are unaware of our powerful acts. We do not consciously pay attention to breathing, pulse rate, or even thoughts and feelings. The student of power is asked to gain control of the movement of energy, and in doing so, become fully conscious of what he or she is accomplishing—and why.

Some people question the difference between momentum and power. A master of momentum knows how to move. A master of power knows which actions—or nonactions—will produce which results, and works deliberately toward a higher goal. To do this, he or she activates the most essential soul qualities: the spiritual gifts.

Affiliation with the Ninth Chakra and Auric Layer

Your ninth chakra holds the "genes of your soul." These are the programs, encrypted as symbols, that form the basis of your soul. When fully activated, these programs enhance your spiritual gifts and attract energies to support your personal destiny. Rhodium is a rare element that assists in attaining higher states of consciousness. In concert with platinum, the transitional metal associated with the thirteenth and highest Plane, rhodium vibrates our soul into spirit status.

Our soul holds all the powers of our spirit. In order to clear karma and express itself dharmically, our soul must make conscious and willful choices about how to *live* love. With ninth chakra energies, the soul is able to catalyze love through power, thus creating more love.

The Wisdom of the Plane of Power

We all have spiritual powers. Upon arriving on this Plane, we are met with a master of power who instantly awakens our spiritual gifts. I discuss these gifts in detail in my book *Attracting Prosperity*

Through the Chakras, showing which chakra houses which gift. In summary, the gifts and abilities are:

- First chakra: Manifestation. Making something out of nothing.
- Second chakra: Creativity. Forming artistry or compassion out of feelings.
- Third chakra: Administration. Organizing information for a higher goal.
- Fourth chakra: Healing. Improving relationships with love.
- Fifth chakra: Communication. Receiving and sharing wisdom.
- Sixth chakra: Visioning. Using visions to strategize and create desirable futures.
- Seventh chakra: Prophecy. Perceiving and working toward divine destiny.
- Eighth chakra: Shamanism. Walking all worlds and dimensions.
- Ninth chakra: Harmonizing. Bringing the world closer to its ideal state.
- Tenth chakra: Naturalism. Enhancing the natural world.
- Eleventh chakra: Commanding. Directing natural and supernatural forces.
- Twelfth chakra: Mastery. Being the self that you truly are.

We all possess at least one of these gifts, which must be activated and practiced on the Plane of Power. What good is a gift unless it is used? What good is a gift unless it is *well* used? On the Plane of Power, masters guide students in finding uses for their gifts, among both the living and those dwelling in the afterlife.

Masters on the Plane of Power

There are countless types of masters on the Plane of Power. Essentially, a student is matched with one of comparable gifts: you cannot learn how to be a carpenter from an expert on birds.

🌿

ANCIENT ONES ON THE PLANE OF POWER

The Plane of Power is a meeting point for the Ancient Ones, the group of souls that helped create the material worlds. From their inception, these souls were highly attuned to the Creator's will and fully vested with their own spiritual gifts. Applying their considerable abilities, they helped conceive the worlds, and even now continue to spin light, enable consciousness, and guide emerging souls to their destinies.

Unfortunately, there is a subset of Ancient Ones that is more enchanted with power than love. They know exactly how to manipulate others toward their own, greedy ends. These are "dark" Ancient Ones, and they serve at cross-purposes to the "light" Ancient Ones.

Dark Ancient Ones want to rule, and if they cannot rule the heavens they will reign on earth. Very few graduate from the Plane of Power, because they empower themselves instead of love. Having cut themselves off from the light—the genesis field that supports all living beings—they have to "steal" others' energy or light to sustain themselves. They do this through malicious and deliberate acts of manipulation, chaos, and violence.

Most dark ones remain in entity form and plague the living—or the just-passed. They are masters at psychic vampirism.

For instance, they might tell a just-departed soul that it is going to hell unless they join forces. They might project nightmares onto a young child, insisting that only they can keep her safe. They might also manipulate the vulnerable into performing cruel or inhumane acts toward others.

Some dark Ancient Ones incarnate repeatedly, searching for more and more power. They often retain full memory of their past lives and complete control of their spiritual gifts. Many end up in religious, political, or cultural leadership roles.

Many light Ancient Ones remain on the Plane of Power—even though they could graduate—to battle the evil of the dark Ancient Ones. Some work in entity form, while others incarnate. Living light helpers are often born with a deep understanding of the conflict between good and evil and often feel compelled to right wrongs. Quite a few construct-soul and indigo-soul children are really Ancient Ones.

Some people believe that certain groups of Ancient Ones have incarnated and will never die. Immortal vampires would qualify as a dark variety; immortal heroes, as the light bearers. It is said that these beings walk among us, perhaps providing the story lines for children's superheroes.

Potential Challenges

The greater our abilities, the greater the temptation to use them for personal rather than collective gain. Consider the lives of most living saints, gurus, and masters. Have you ever wondered why they so seldom use their abilities to become rich, famous, or even healthy? Yogananda, a yogi master, had back pain throughout his life. Edgar Cayce, a Christian channeler and healer, died young. The apostle Paul spoke of an affliction that never went away. Yet, each of these living beings of light could heal and help other people.

The greatest lesson of love is that love is not about perfection. We are not masters of power because we have ideal lives, ideal bodies, or mansions all over the world. We are masters of power when we use our gifts to create more wholeness for others and ourselves. Is a crippled person less than whole? Is a child with Down syndrome a lesser being than a child with genius-level intelligence? It's tempting—but not practical—to fix something just because we can (or think we can).

The Plane of Power — For the Living

How do you achieve a comfortable relationship with power without falling prey to its many temptations? Here are a few ideas:

- *Ask for a power guide.* Ask the Divine to send you
  an Ancient One to offer insight about choices and
  consequences of action. How would you recognize this
  person or nonhuman guide? To the visually psychic,
  an Ancient One might appear as a person, but if you
  peer into the auric field around this guide you will
  detect swirls of white, black, and gray energies—forces
  ready to be commanded. An Ancient One will speak

with authority and conviction, and you will sense its commanding presence. You can always ask this or any entity to tell you who and what it is and if it works "for the light" or not. A power guide will:

Emphasize nonaction over action, to avoid wielding power inappropriately or interfering with another's destiny.

Ask questions. They will not tell you what to do; they will help you determine a plan of action.

Help you learn from your errors.

Never demand that you follow them, that instead you follow the Divine. They will help you develop your spiritual gifts and use them for a higher purpose.

- *Study power.* Much of history is a review of acts of power. Look for positive examples among famous people of all cultures, then create your own ethical criteria for the use of power.

- *Make love your touchstone.* Before you act, ask yourself if your behavior will increase or decrease love.

- *Get an accountability friend.* It's helpful to work with someone else to review what you have done, how you have felt about it, and what you want to do in the future.

- *Energetically.* Use the color gold psychically to help you harmonize with higher energies. Wear gold, or use your intention to program your gold jewelry to attract wisdom and power. Concentrate on rhodium when meditating to attune your ninth chakra to the Plane of Power. One method for accessing rhodium's empowering energies is to create a rhodium mirror. Rhodium is silver-white and reflective and is often used to coat other metals. It also stimulates the dream state. A rhodium mirror is a perfect vehicle for activating your imagination and opening to universal powers. When issues of power arise, visualize a mirror made of rhodium (or designate any handheld mirror as your "rhodium" mirror and use that instead) and ask to see ways to handle the challenge. Ask that the forces or energies you need in order to act with confidence enter your ninth chakra through this mirror, which can serve as an information provider but also as a portal between worlds.

CHAPTER 18

THE ELEVENTH PLANE: THE PLANE OF CHARITY

CHAKRA Eleventh, a skein inside the twelfth auric field, especially condensed around the hands and feet.

AURA Eleventh auric field, interwoven with the eleventh chakra, inside the twelfth field.

CHAKRIC COLOR Rose.

CHAKRIC GLAND Connective tissue.

CHAKRIC ELEMENT Indium, which stabilizes the hypothalamus and the pituitary glands through its bonding with salts, thus supporting and balancing the physical body.

Overview of the Plane of Charity

Many people believe that love and charity are the same thing. They are related, it's true, yet there are differences. Love is unconditional. It is the material that makes up everything in the world. Charity is equivalent to grace: it is love plus power, or lovingness. When we mix these two ingredients, much as a baker does flour and water, we get sustenance: the bread that feeds the soul and the body.

Charitable people do not go searching for charitable acts to perform. They meet the needs presented them in everyday life. Maybe a son or daughter needs a pep talk or some baseball coaching or help with homework. Perhaps a friend needs someone to listen or a place to stay. By the time a soul has reached the level of charity, it has developed its own individual set of skills. If it operates in accordance with what provides it pleasure and a sense of purpose, it will naturally become a force of goodwill.

So what makes being charitable different from just "being good"? Being charitable has a lot in common with *being* good and *looking* good, but the motivation isn't about goodness—it's purely about helping others through impartiality.

Someone interested in being or looking good will give others what they say they need. But charity is an impartial love. The charitable person looks beneath the surface of another's request to the real need beneath it. For example, a poverty-stricken mother might need money to pay a bill, and a "good person" might provide cash. A master of charity might instead perceive that what she really requires is a good job, and deliver employment that pays well.

Affiliation with the Eleventh Chakra and Auric Field

The eleventh chakra and auric field combine to form a rose-colored band inside the twelfth auric field. This chakra is associated with the ability to command natural and supernatural forces. The auric field wields this power and also filters beneficial forces from harmful ones.

If we are open to the wisdom of charity, or grace, these forces will create health, structural well-being, vitality, and a powerful presence. Indium, the transitional metal associated with this chakra, boosts our hormonal system overall, and specifically the hypothalamus. This may be the "antiaging" miracle that so many people are looking for.

The Wisdom of Grace

Grace is the gift of love that finds us when we do not think we are worthy of it. Masters of charity are conduits for grace. They are able to grant wishes, blessings, and goodwill for others. Masters of charity can do this because they know that the ultimate power — love — does not start with them. It emanates from the Divine. Whether or not they know the perfect technique for healing or know how to yield the right brushstroke for a masterpiece, masters of charity know that since everything is love, what they need, for themselves or others, will be provided. All they have to do is ask.

Masters on the Plane of Charity

If you visit this Plane, you will meet many of the people illuminated in famous paintings, images of the saints, and iconography — maybe even in baseball paraphernalia! At some level, all these beings exist on the Plane of Charity, perhaps not in exact form, but in energetic equivalency. Even if there is not exactly a "jinn of good luck" or a being that would call itself Ganesh of the Hindu faith, there will be souls that are equal in mind, deed, and capability.

Most angels, Forms, Shining Ones, Powers, Cherubim, Seraphim, and the like spend considerable time on the Plane of Charity. They do not need to do good works to qualify as holy: they do so because they truly enjoy giving.

Potential Challenges

It never pays to be "too good." The most frequent mistake "want-to-be" charity masters make is thinking that they need to be perfect—charitable all the time.

Think about the challenges of being a paragon of charity. It's easy to think of Mother Teresa. Flawlessly and tirelessly, she served the sick, the displaced, and the needy. I would like to think that once in a while she had a laugh over a beer with a good friend or indulged in a cheery movie. Through my profession, I have met amazing human beings, many devoted selflessly to helping others through their chosen fields. And while others praise them, I always first ask the question: "Would this person still qualify as a *real person?*"

There's no excuse for losing our "realness." No matter how elevated or saintly we become, humility is key to higher consciousness. We can remain humble by remaining in touch with our own personal needs. How can we be vulnerable enough to help others if we don't retain our own vulnerability? How can we be compassionate toward the weaknesses of others if we conceal our own?

I am often shocked by the hidden side of the most touted "spiritual" individuals. I don't think less of them for their secret affairs, addictions, money problems, or prejudices. I simply think, as I do when encountering these same weaknesses in others, "Why do they do this to themselves?"

Why would we withhold love from ourselves? This is the end result of ignoring our personal needs and issues. Charity begins and ends with the self. We must accept love if we are to be loving. We must then use love to empower lovingness. Student souls on the Plane of Charity face these and other questions under the guidance of masters of charity.

The Plane of Charity — For the Living

Here are some ways to be charitable — and still enjoy life.

- *Connect with a saint, one connected with your preferred religion.* There are deities, demigods, saints, natural spirits . . . a plethora of people and energies. At some level, most of them exist on the Plane of Charity. Determine which attributes you most want to develop or encourage, and ask for help from that being.
- *Open your eyes: needs abound!* Offer your gifts.
- *Invite help.* Experience the gratitude inherent in receiving from others. Ask your spiritual guides and the people around you for help.
- *Try gratitude first.* Some spiritually oriented people have told me to be grateful for what you want to receive, even before it comes. This is spiritual manipulation. Instead, be grateful for what already exists. Want a bigger car? Be happy that you *have* a car.

- *Be filled with grace.* Try forgiveness. People don't usually hurt others intentionally; they make mistakes. Give others the benefit of the doubt, and you will be happier—and have more friends.
- *Do not make excuses for inaction.* If someone needs help, don't wait for someone else to respond.
- *Energetically.* Concentrate on the appropriate use of your powers. Get in touch with your special abilities to manifest or manage natural or supernatural forces. Image the color pink and, with intention, ask the Divine to stimulate the appropriate levels of indium in your system, so that you can become a recipient of—and conduit for—grace.

CHAPTER 19

THE TWELFTH PLANE: THE PLANE OF MASTERY

CHAKRA Twelfth, a bubble around the eleventh chakra, serving as the outer container for the human self. Inserts into thirty-two secondary chakra points in the body.

AURA Twelfth auric field, interspersed with the chakra around the eleventh auric field.

CHAKRIC COLOR Clear.

CHAKRIC GLAND The thirty-two secondary chakra points— stimulates the endocrine functions within all cells, organs, and joints.

CHAKRIC ELEMENT Osmium, bringing in interdimensional and planetary energies.

Overview of the Plane of Mastery

What does it mean to be a master? The word *mastery* refers to expert knowledge or outstanding ability. Therefore, a master has expertise in a body of knowledge and finesse at a set of skills. But that's just the beginning of the story.

There are four qualities, or virtues, that reveal true mastery. These are described in various approaches to becoming a spiritual warrior, an Eastern concept of heroism. They include:

- *Fearlessness:* Complete knowledge of your own weaknesses and strengths.
- *Courage:* The ability to stretch beyond current boundaries in order to achieve higher results.
- *Honor:* The upholding of higher values, even under adverse conditions.
- *Humor:* The ability to see the grace in all situations.

A master is really made from the inside out.

Affiliation with the Twelfth Chakra and Auric Field

The twelfth chakra and auric field marry to create the boundary between the human and the Divine selves, the earth and the planetary systems, and the personal and universal realms. Osmium is a higher metal that translates interdimensional energies into the physical world, and so cultivates the spirit within the body. Consider that the twelfth chakra works through thirty-two secondary bodily chakra points, as well as within the cells. Osmium — mastery — brings the heavens to earth, and directly into our own bodies. For the living, mastership intrinsically relies upon the acceptance and enjoyment of the physical body, not just an assumption of higher consciousness.

The Wisdom of the Plane of Mastery

Most people think that masters are people who are good at something. They might be, but that is not the only criterion. To evolve into a true master is to gain understanding of—and to fully express—the four mastership virtues. Most important, one must also resist the twin temptations of perfectionism and taking oneself too seriously. Ironically, we can't completely master anything, because we always have more to learn. If we're fearless, we accept our weaknesses even while cultivating our strengths. If we're courageous, we work on our weaknesses, even though we might never completely succeed at transforming them. If we're honorable, we uphold higher ideals, even though we fall short of them. And if we have a sense of humor, we can laugh at ourselves for thinking that we are masters at all, and still have fun being good at what we do.

Masters on the Plane of Mastery

A student of mastery has no true "masters"; instead he or she has "master peers" who might serve as friends, companions, and confidantes. Each mastery student, however, is linked with a Watcher, which serves as witness to the soul's process. Watchers cannot interfere or provide instruction. On this Plane they do, however, perform a very interesting function. They return a mastery student to his or her most challenging incarnation. Here, the student might actually reoccupy the original body or watch as if from afar, depending upon the situation.

There are many reasons for returning a student of mastery to the past. First, reviewing past behavior invokes the lessons of every other Plane of Light traversed. From the Plane of Rest: can we simply accept that what has happened, has happened? From the Plane of Evaluation: can we review a difficulty with pure compassion? And so on we go—with a new twist. What happens when we mix teachings? For instance, can we apply power to healing? Charitable grace to momentum? On the Mastery Plane, the student must integrate every teaching to ultimately make a decision: Would he or she really change the past or not? If so, how? Most important, why?

The second theme of this Plane concerns time. When we are alive, time is extremely hard to comprehend. We think it is a series of ticks and tocks that march ever forward. We're so used to living by the clock: setting our alarms, counting the years to determine our age, evaluating our days by how much time we spend doing something enjoyable versus something laborious. But then, we think that death follows life and that the two are separate, don't we? Interdimensionally, time is malleable—and differs from Plane to Plane. The student of mastery must engage fully in the process of "real time" or the *eternal present,* in which every moment of the past, present, and future is fully engaged with all others. What we did affects the present and therefore the future; what we are doing alters the past and the present; and what will be shapes everything else. By visiting the past, the student of mastery is forced to struggle with this confusion. If he or she alters the past, what might happen to the present and the future, for self and others? According to the laws of physics, the mere observation of the past creates a change. What is the student going to do about that?

While we are alive, it's just as challenging to understand space, which is not as ordinary as earthlings might have it. As I've already suggested in our discussion of quantum physics, an object (or soul) can occupy two or more places at the same time, and two or more objects can coexist within the exact same space. This means that a mastery student can dwell on the Mastery Plane and be back on earth—in any time period or already-occupied body—at the same time.

At any given time, there are countless mastery students on this planet. They might be accountants or janitors, homemakers or children, but they have clothed themselves in skin and humanity to "practice what they preach." The Watcher stands by as a loving witness to the mastery student, who must ask him- or herself some pretty challenging questions:

- Should I alter the past?
- Should I talk with my former incarnation?
- Should I show my former incarnation what is going to happen if it doesn't change?
- Should I ignore everything and leave the past alone?
- Bottom line—should I intervene or not? And if so, how?

Potential Challenges

By participating in his or her own past, the mastery student is learning hands-on how to be a spiritual guide—for him- or herself. He or she is presented the opportunity to integrate the perspective of every Plane and make choices that create real consequences. Presumably, a master will affect the entire universe: how will he or she make decisions that will shift the past, the present, and the future? There's no one watching except a Watcher, and the Watcher is sworn to silence. Think how strong the temptation will be to simply make it easier for the past self, or to take away the sting of certain lessons by avoiding the corresponding events altogether. Would you prevent an abuse that could spare your past self years of pain if you would then fail to develop courage or compassion? What if in the future this compassion would enable you to assist hundreds of needy people? Inevitably, the mastery student must examine what fearlessness, courage, honor, and humor mean in human-life situations—across time and space.

The Plane of Mastery — For the Living

A living master continually cultivates the four virtues. Here are some ways we can do this:

- *Fearlessness.* Fearlessness is not the same as being without fear. Fear is useful; it helps us know what direction to take—or avoid. Being fearless begins and ends with not being afraid of ourselves. If you are serious about learning about yourself, you might want to take notes. Really. Pretend you are your own mother. We have all seen mothers as they watch their children and notice the tiniest burp or skin blotch, or the subtlest smile. What might you learn if you played the part of your own Divine mother and scrutinized yourself this closely?
- *Courage.* The courageous person has a big heart. He or she is not without fear, any more than is the fearless person. Courage involves facing danger or uncertainty

with a heart that is wide open instead of half-shut. When our heart is open, we love without conditions; and it stays open no matter how we are treated. An open heart is a channel for grace, for the Divine flow of love and power that cannot be generated by our own being.

You practice courage by ignoring shame, as we learned on the Plane of Healing. Decide not to let it cloud your vision. Play Divine father and coach yourself forward in life. Keep telling yourself how great you are at something—and get out there and do it. That is all it takes to be courageous.

- *Honor.* Every day presents us with opportunities to be honorable instead of dishonorable. Honor involves standing up for something or someone even at a cost. Honor is not about conducting a crusade; it is about the small activities in life. Outline your values and pick one or two that are most important—and then live them.

- *Humor.* Have you ever met a completely humorless person? Did you like spending time with him or her? Most people take themselves too seriously, at least some of the time. When we do this, we become self-involved and fail to read others—as well as ourselves—with accuracy. Humor lends perspective, as well as the lightness of heart and being that invites an easy approach to problem solving. Humor is the quality of something that elicits amusement. And life is pretty amusing.

- *Energetically.* Concentrate on the element of osmium, sensing this spinning metal in your outer field, as well as throughout your body. Osmium is extremely dense and presents as blue-gray or blue-black. To work with it, you might visualize a shimmering field of either shade of blue and imagine it surrounding you, connecting your twelfth chakra and auric field with the greater universe. Know yourself as bigger than your body—and made of love. As you practice this awareness, it becomes true.

The living mastery student must live in the past and present simultaneously while keeping an eye on the ever-evolving future. How do you do this?

- *Return to the Planes of Evaluation and Healing, if necessary.* Take yet another walk through your past. Are you stuck anywhere? Are there old beliefs preventing current happiness and joy? Apply the wisdom of forgiveness where appropriate.
- *Return to the Plane of Love.* We can all gain the ability to maneuver time and space; the key is love. Everything is made of love. This means that even the cruelest heart contains a grain of love and the ability to make a loving choice; the most painful of experiences is a learning about love. If you can find the germ of love and enhance it, you can create a new future, and even a new past and present! To practice this theory, spend time figuring out how the worst times in your life have transformed (or can be reconfigured) into the most important times in your life. And then greet the day promising to seek only

the love centered within all the people you meet and situations you face.

- *Work to rid yourself of the notions of past, present, and future.* Embrace life as an "All." You live at all times, in all spaces. What you do now certainly affects the future, but your "future self," your mastery self, can help you make effective decisions today.

- *Let life amuse you.* Humor is really the key.

CHAPTER 20

LOCATING YOURSELF
ON THE PLANES OF LIGHT

*There were also two true mirrors that were out-
side the Master of Mirror's control and had never
been contaminated by him, and if Oliver could
find them — well, that would be good, but why
exactly? And what made a mirror "true"?*

ADAM GOPNIK
THE KING IN THE WINDOW

Do you remember any of your in-between lives, the times
between incarnations? Which felt familiar? Which quick-
ened your interests, inspired you to visit the Planes? Which Plane
seems to be presenting the issues of interest today?

During or in between lives, we have all experienced at least a
few of the Planes of Light. The following guided meditation is an
invitation into your soul's memory bank. It has been designed to
slip you into the recesses of your dream mind, the place that stores
the knowledge of everything you have experienced — on earth and
in the afterlife. You can use this meditation to recollect what you

have learned in between lives, to figure out which Plane you might be working on now, and to stimulate the light that will pull you forward into your true self.

The Meditation into the Mirror

I encourage you to read through this meditation, then close your eyes and experience it silently. You can also tape it for yourself and play it back, or ask a friend to read it to you.

Close your eyes and focus on your breathing. "Breath" and "spirit" mean the same thing in Greek, Hebrew, and Latin. Know that every time you breathe, you are acknowledging the spirit that you are, as well as the Greater Spirit. Accept that your own spirit will keep you safe during this process, providing you with all the information you need.

As you relax, bring your consciousness into your heart. The heart is the center of the body, and it is here that you are able to perceive everything truthfully and wholly. As you alight within, you discover that you can see, hear, and perceive intuitively. It is as if all your senses are alive—and not only in the third dimension, but in all of them.

Gold light surrounds you, and you find yourself in a crystal cave deep within your own heart. You can see the two white tunnels of death

leading away, but angels guard them, for it is not your time. Instead, you bring your focus to a silver mirror, which is right in front of you.

This is the Mirror of Light. It shines brightly, and yet you can still perceive images and pictures in it. As you look into it, you ask a question—and see a response! This mirror will show you everything you need to know, with absolute truth.

Clear the mirror with your mind and ask this question: What Plane of Light did I visit right before this life?

Pause, and observe the answer. After a while, you may ask more questions of the mirror. Did I graduate? Who was my master? What did I learn? What service did I perform during that time? How is this wisdom impacting me during this lifetime?

When you are done asking about where you have been, clear the mirror with intention, and then ask the following: Which Plane have I been working on? Follow-up questions might include, What have I learned? What is incomplete? If you sense that you are finished with this Plane, you might inquire, Which Plane should I focus on at this time in my life?

Ask other questions that are pertinent, such as, What master would the Divine like to assign me? How should I live the wisdom of the Plane I'm on — or the Planes I've graduated from?

When you are finished, slip a black curtain over the mirror. This mirror is yours. You can return to it anytime you want. Gather your thoughts, and before you leave the crystal cave, decide if you would like to drink a little of the gold energy from the heart. This is a higher metal — a living, conscious energy that can keep you connected to your heart and to Divine love. Bathe in it, sip it, and enjoy it before concentrating once again on your breathing. As you return to full consciousness, keep your eyes closed for a moment, enjoying the gold energy in and around you. And then, when you are ready, return to everyday life.

CHAPTER 21

THE "THIRTEENTH PLANE": AN INVITATION INTO ONLY LIGHT

Elinor should have built her world around Jenny when Saul died in that accident on a road outside Boston, but instead she walked into the garden and she had never come out again . . . Here, at least you could make something grow. Here what you buried arose once more, given the correct amounts of sunlight and fertilizer and rain.

ALICE HOFFMAN
THE PROBABLE FUTURE

As a master, you have decided to live the light that is your true self. You understand that life is the same as death; both involve reveling on the river of light. You know that everything is—and has been—what it needs to be for your higher development. As "perfect" as your "imperfection" has been, you know that a true master constantly works to improve the journey, as well as his or her attitude about it.

You have willingly undertaken the slow, arduous work of making peace with your past, the task of the lower Planes. You have actively pursued your passions, transforming your world into a place of worship. This is the duty of the middle Planes. You have been sharing your light with others, the joy of the upper Planes. And now you are ready for more, but you don't know what that means.

You are ready to complete your evolution—not by turning back into the spirit you were, oh, millennia ago. The past cannot repeat. You can't "go home again"—but you don't need to. The eons spent devolving during your lifetimes have been offset and transformed by the eons spent evolving through the afterlife. You have become more than you ever were.

Life and the Planes of Light have taught compassion, forgiveness, truth, and wisdom. You've learned what love—and power, charity, and mastery—really are.

You've triumphed over fear, hatred, and greed. You didn't do this through anger, retribution, or judgment, although these were useful tools for learning. At some point, you understood that you could just as easily exchange a smile for rage, or hand out flower blossoms instead of negative words. Hunger resulted in an appreciation for warm bread and butter; cruelty called forth courage. And death—lifetimes of death—has certainly taught you that there is nothing to fear. There is no loss. There is no separation. There is only the continuation of self and others. As twin experiences, life and death revealed you to yourself.

In your mastery, you begin to notice yet another Plane of existence, a freshly emerging level of awareness. You might call it the "Thirteenth Plane," for it follows the wisdom gathering of the other Planes. And yet, it is available to anyone at any time—for it is really a Plane of self. It is a Plane unique and personal to you: it is a consciousness that embraces all you've ever been, have done, and might become. You won't experience this Plane the same as others might, for this Plane is you — and it is light.

Jesus once said, "I am the way, the truth, and the light." To reach the "Thirteenth Plane" is to comprehend these words. He *is* the way, the truth, and the light — of himself, just as you are the way, the truth, and the light of yourself.

For a caterpillar to metamorphose, every organ must break down. Before the cells can shift to their new sites — before the wings can form — the caterpillar literally turns to mush. The butterfly only emerges after this long process of death and dying. At no time is the caterpillar any less a butterfly. Once emerged, at no time is the butterfly any less a caterpillar. They are one and the same.

Through your many incarnations and exits, you've become the same as the caterpillar-butterfly. You have feet with which to tramp the ground and wings with which to fly. Can you use both? Are you willing? Then you qualify for the "Thirteenth Plane" of Light: pure consciousness, the living of the light of self. You need concentrate on only one main activity: traveling the conjoined river of death and life, which you now know how to do.

You grasp your oars — and row.

CONCLUSION: FULLY ALIVE ON THE PLANES OF LIGHT

Though he was the ultimate Kwisatz Haderach with immeasurable power, Duncan had known the best parts of being human. Life after life. He didn't need to feel alienated and worried, when he could be filled with love instead . . .

And Duncan Idaho was greater than the flesh that encompassed his body.

BRIAN HERBERT AND KEVIN J. ANDERSON
SANDWORMS OF DUNE

You have now explored the Planes of the afterlife, the bands of light that provide illumination and wisdom in death and in life. You've glimpsed the garden of rest and restoration, visited the havens of wisdom, power, and charity, and asked yourself what it is that you want to master. This journey, however, as eye-opening as it may have been, is make-believe; you've been reading about it in a book. The question is: how will you live it?

Perhaps you've done some of the exercises in these chapters and have already incorporated your discoveries into your life. Maybe you've wandered in between lives or on certain Planes and learned from your experiences. If so, you are finishing this book a different person from the one who first opened it; you are more thoroughly *you*—the genuine, luminescent spirit that you are.

What would it mean to continue your life in this way, as a seeker who has found? As the river walker who has not only seen his or her own death, but who yearns to live the truths of the Planes of Light?

To embrace the wisdom of the Planes is to stop fearing death—and life. It is to acknowledge the instruction and powers forthcoming from the Planes and to use them now, not only in the afterlife. To be this alive would be to enhance the best of being human and to live completely.

How can you be the "best possible human"? Accessing the Planes is like having a universal remote—a magical one. You can tune in to any channel you desire in an instant and, better still, press a button and materialize the teacher, information, or energy that you need. This newfound power could create a temptation to do whatever *you* want.

If you aren't afraid of hell, you can enjoy being such a heathen. If you can call forth entities, knowledge, and forces, you can snap your fingers for wealth and probably get it. You can attract a glamorous relationship or write a best-selling book. After all, if you can direct the energies of death, you can control what happens in your life.

But is this really the best use of the light of the Planes? For a moment, shift from thinking about the Planes themselves and what you can do with their energies, and concentrate on the *meaning* of the *existence* of the Planes. If the Planes exist—and I believe that they do—then it means that "something," "somewhere" loved us enough to create them. Something, somewhere designed a learning path for our souls. And countless masters and beings of light have agreed to make available — and palatable — the wisdom of the Planes, to help us on the river of death and life even to the point of rowing our boat when we are too tired to do it for ourselves. Ask yourself, why would someone do this? More important, why would this someone do this for *you*?

Because you are lovable and loved.

Because you are deserving and terrific.

Because, like the helpers and the Chief Designer, you are also a being of light and need only the illumination provided in the step-by-step progression of the Planes to realize it.

Because you *are* a "Kwisatz Haderach" and are worthy of the time and attention needed to help you achieve your personal destiny.

What does it mean to be a Kwisatz Haderach? The stories in the *Dune* science fiction series span thousands of years, and throughout the series, readers eagerly anticipate the second and final Kwisatz Haderach, a prophesized Christ figure. All of the other characters yearn to be rescued from the mess they have made in their personal lives and in the universe as a whole, so there is a great sigh of relief when the Kwisatz Haderach is found. He is Duncan, a clone who remembers everything he has ever experienced and learned in his many past incarnations. More important, he remembers what he has learned and achieved in every state of being.

We might say that Duncan has graduated from the Planes of Light. He now embodies the wisdom of each and has "risen" into illuminated consciousness. What will he do with his powers? Rescue everyone? No, it is clear that he intends to serve as a guide, not a savior. Will he revel in his self-importance and fulfill only his own desires — or perhaps do the opposite, and establish himself as a god, now that he no longer needs to be human? No in both cases. As the book relates, "His would not be a conventional kind of love. His love needed to extend much farther, to every living person, and to thinking machines." Despite his transcended state, Duncan chooses to retain his humanity and humility — and simply love. To love in the way that makes a difference in the world.

You don't have to die to achieve transcendence. You needn't do all of the exercises in this book or graduate from each Plane of Light with an "A." You don't have to be perfect or give up chocolate or never be grumpy again. All you really need is to know this:

The world needs your love.
The world needs you.

In fact, it might need you more than you need a new car or a bigger house, more than you need greater patience or a different job. It might need you just the way you are.

This is the true message of the Planes of Light, the wisdom illuminated by each and every Plane. You are light, and your light is unique and special. Your light is needed to transform the world into what it is supposed to be: a community of lights.

But your worth is also greater than what you are able to provide for others. If you were the only being in existence, the Source would still love you enough to establish the entirety of the Planes — just so you could recognize the truth of who you are. You are so loved that the All has created the Planes not only to "save" you from death, but also to encourage you to embrace life everlasting. This eternity exists whether you are alive or in soul form, and whether you know it or not.

What if you could fully embrace this fact and live at the intersection of life and death, as a master of the Planes and a master of life? What might it mean to live in this transcended state? You could get whatever you wish for—but even better, know what is best to wish for. You could help others—and even better, help them help themselves. You could expand beyond the bounds of flesh—and even better, enjoy each moment of having a body. You could be the Kwisatz Haderach you were meant to be.

Each lifetime has led you to this one. May you be the light that you are. May you know that this light is made of love, and be the loving and enlightened one the Source already knows you to be.

NOTES

Introduction

1. Holger Kalweit, *Dreamtime & Inner Space* (Boston: Shambhala, 1988), 3.

Chapter 1

1. Thomas E. Mails, *Fools Crow: Wisdom and Power* (Tulsa, OK: Council Oak Books, 1991), 136.

2. Paul Brunton, Ph.D., *The Wisdom of the Overself* (New York: Samuel Weiser, 1972), 52.

Chapter 2

1. Richard Gerber, M.D., *Vibrational Medicine* (Santa Fe, NM: Bear & Co., 1988), 162.

2. Ibid., 484.

3. Gershon Winkler, *Magic of the Ordinary* (Berkeley, CA: North Atlantic Books, 2003), 94.

4. Mircea Eliade, *The Sacred and the Profane* (New York: Harcourt Brace Jovanovich, 1959), 176.

5. Lynne McTaggart, *The Field* (New York: Harper Perennial, 2001), 49–53.

6. Michael A. Cremo, *Human Devolution* (Los Angeles: Bhaktivedanta Book Publishing, 2003), 483.

7. Gerber, *Vibrational Medicine*, 488.

8. Ibid., 418.

Chapter 3

1. Malidoma Patrice Somé, *Of Water and the Spirit* (New York: The Penguin Group, 1994), 192.

2. George Gallup, Jr., *Adventures in Immortality* (New York: McGraw-Hill, 1982), 422.

3. http://en.wikipedia.org/wiki/Near_death_experience (accessed June 2007).

4. Gallup, *Adventures in Immortality*, 422.

5. Dannion Brinkley, with Paul Perry, *Saved by the Light* (New York: HarperCollins, 1994), 95–96.

6. Janis Amatuzio, M.D., *Forever Ours* (Novato, CA: New World Library, 2002), 183.

7. Brinkley with Perry, *Saved by the Light*, xiii.

8. http://www.firethegrid.org/eng/home-fr-eng.htm (accessed July 20, 2007).

9. Paul Brunton, Ph.D., *The Quest of the Overself* (New York: Samuel Weiser, 1975), 153.

10. Gary Zukav, *The Seat of the Soul* (New York: Fireside, 1990), 186.

11. Rita Carter, *Mapping the Mind* (Los Angeles: University of California Press, 1998), 13.

12. Ibid., 13.

13. Melvin Morse, M.D., and Paul Perry, *Transformed by the Light* (New York: Random House, 1992), 146.

Chapter 4

1. Paul Pearsall, Ph.D., *The Heart's Code* (New York: Broadway Books, 1988), 13.
2. http://ndewton.dep.anl.give/archieve.htm (accessed September 2007).
3. Seth Lloyd, *Programming the Universe* (New York: Vintage Books, 2006), 69.
4. Ibid., 68.
5. Michael Talbot, *The Holographic Universe* (New York: HarperCollins, 1991), 275–276.
6. Ibid., 67.

Chapter 5

1. Reed Karaim, "Light That Can Cure You," Special Health Report: Caring for Aging Parents, Health, *USA Weekend,* February 4, 2007.
2. Lene Hau Vestergaard, "Frozen Light," *Scientific American,* May 2003, 44–51.
3. McTaggart, *The Field,* 95.
4. Ibid., 44–51.
5. Valerie V. Hunt, "Appendix, The Rolf Study," in Rosalyn L. Bruyere, *Wheels of Light* (Arcadia, CA: Bon Productions, 1989), 247–258.

Chapter 6

1. William Shakespeare, *Hamlet,* I.v., 166–167.
2. Laurence Gardner, *Lost Secrets of the Sacred Ark* (New York: Barnes and Noble, 2003), 10–25.
3. Ibid., 163–64. More information is available from http://www.nigms.nih.gov/news/meetings/metals.html
4. Hal E. Puthoff, "Gravity as a Zero-Point Fluctuation Force," *Physical Review A* 39, no. 5, 1989.
5. Mark Alpert, "The Triangular Universe," *Scientific American,* February 2007, 24.

Special Section

1. William Smith, L.L.D., *Smith's Bible Dictionary* (1868 revised) (Nashville, TN: Thomas Nelson, 2004).
2. Gerber, *Vibrational Medicine,* 493.
3. Betty J. Eadie, *Embraced by the Light* (New York: Bantam Books, 1994), 66.
4. James Van Praagh, *Talking to Heaven* (New York: Signet, 1999), 62–70.
5. W.C. Langer, *The Mind of Adolf Hitler: The Secret Wartime Diaries* (New York: Basic Books, 1972), 34, as referenced in Stevan J. Thayer and Linda Sue Nathanson, Ph.D., *Interview with an Angel* (New York: Dell Publishing, 1997), 50–51.

Chapter 7

1. Joel L. Whitton, and Joe Fisher, *Life Between Life* (New York: Doubleday, 1986), 35.

2. Talbot, *The Holographic Universe*, 215.

3. Michael Newton, Ph.D., *Journey of Souls* (St. Paul, MN: Llewellyn Publications, 1996).

4. Max Freedom Long, *The Secret Science Behind Miracles* (Marina del Rey, CA: DeVorss Publications, 1976), 396–400.

5. Ibid.

BIBLIOGRAPHY

Aczel, Amir D. *Entanglement.* New York: Penguin, 2001.

Alpert, Mark. "The Triangular Universe." *Scientific American,* February 2007, 24.

Amatuzio, Janis, M.D. *Forever Ours.* Novato, CA: New World Library, 2002.

Attanasio, A. A. *The Serpent and the Grail.* New York: HarperPrism, 1999.

Bartlett, Richard, D.C., N.D. *Matrix Energetics.* New York: Atria Books, 2007.

Bear, Jaya. *Amazon Magic.* El Prado, NM: Colibri Publishing, 2000.

Begley, Sharon. *Train Your Mind, Change Your Brain.* New York: Ballantine, 2007.

Boutin, Chad. "Bright Idea Could Doom Cancer and Viruses, Says Purdue Scientists." *Purdue University News,* August 23, 2004. Based on an abstract by Elton L. Menon, Rushika Perera, Maribel Navarro, Richard J. Kuhn, and Harry Morrison. "Phototoxicity Against Tumor Cells and Sindbis Virus by an Octahedral Rhodium Bisbipyridyl Complex and Evidence for the Genome as a Target in the Viral Photoinactivation." Available at www.purdue.edu/UNS/

html4ever/2004/040824.Morrison.rhodium.html (accessed August 2007).

Boyd, Doug, media contact. "Twin Beginnings Usually Result In Single Births, Researcher Says." *Health Sciences News,* October 9, 2003, Office of News & Information, ECU Division of Health Sciences, www.ecu.edu/dhs/news/newsstory .cfm?ID=115 (accessed July 2007).

Brinkley, Dannion. *The Secrets of the Light.* Henderson, NV: Heart Light Productions, 2004.

Brinkley, Dannion, with Paul Perry. *Saved by the Light.* New York: HarperCollins, 1994.

Browne, Sir Thomas. *The Garden of Cyrus,* 1658. http://thinkexist. com/quotes/thomas_browne,_sr./. Full text available at http:// penelope.uchicago.edu/hgc.html (accessed May 2007).

Brunton, Paul, Ph.D. *The Wisdom of the Overself.* New York: Samuel Weiser, 1972.

Budge, E. A. Wallis. *The Egyptian Book of the Dead, The Papyrus of Ani.* New York: Dover Publications, 1967.

Campbell, Joseph. *The Hero with a Thousand Faces.* Princeton, NJ: Princeton University Press, 1968.

Carter, Rita. *Mapping the Mind.* Berkeley: University of California Press, 1999.

Cassidy, David C. "Heisenberg, Uncertainty, and the Quantum Revolution." *Scientific American,* May 1992, 106–112.

Castaneda, Carlos. *The Active Side of Infinity.* New York: Harper Perennial, 1998.

Chiao, Raymond, Paul G. Kwiat, and Aephraim M. Steinberg. "Faster Than Light?" *Scientific American,* August 1993, 52–60.

Cohen, Jarrett. "Magnetism in the Universe," *Access,* Fall 1995, http://access.ncsa.uiuc.edu/Archive/backissues/95.3/Magnetism.html (accessed July 2007).

Coleman, Graham, ed. *The Tibetan Book of the Dead.* New York: Penguin, 2005.

Cooper, J. C. *Chinese Alchemy.* New York: Sterling, 1990.

Cooper, Roger, (author) and John Erickson (photographer). *Impressions.* Brainerd, MN: Evergreen Press, 2002.

Cott, Jonathan. *The Search for Omm Sety.* New York: Warner, 1987.

Cowan, James G. *Messengers of the Gods.* New York: Bell Tower, 1993.

Cremo, Michael A. *Human Devolution.* Los Angeles: Bhaktivedanta Book Publishing, 2003.

Dallas, Robert E., Ph.D. *A Preliminary Inquiry into the Biological and Neurophysiological Effects of Etherium Gold.* The Mind Spa, June 2, 1998. www.newhuman.co.uk/mindspareport.html (accessed June 2007).

Doresse, Jean. *The Secret Books of the Egyptian Gnostics.* New York: MJF Books, 1986.

Eadie, Betty J. *Embraced by the Light.* New York: Bantam, 1994.

Eliade, Mircea. *The Sacred and the Profane.* New York: Harcourt, Brace & World, 1959.

———. *Shamanism.* Princeton, NJ: Princeton University Press, 1974.

Faulkner, Raymond, trans. *Ancient Egyptian Book of the Dead.* New York: Barnes & Noble, 2005.

Fujiwara, N. H., and D. F. Kallmes. "Healing Response in Elastase-Induced Rabbit Aneurysms After Embolization with a New Platinum Coil System." Department of Radiology, University of Virginia Health Services,

Charlottesville, VA. PMID: 12169470 PubMED — indexed
for MEDLINE. www.ncbi.nlm.nih.gov/entrez/query.fcgi
. Retrieve&db=PubMed&list_uids=12169470&dopt=Abstract
(accessed September 2007).

Gallup, George, Jr. *Adventures in Immortality.* New York:
McGraw-Hill, 1982.

Gardner, Laurence. *Lost Secrets of the Sacred Ark.* New York:
Element, 2004.

Gensler, W. "Tissue Electropotentials in Kalanchoe Blossfeldiana
During Wound Healing." *American Journal of Botany,*
65, no. 2, 152–157. http://links.jstor.org/sici?sici=0002-
9122(197802)65:2%3C152:TEIKBD%3E2.0.CO;2-D
(accessed June 2007).

Gerber, Richard, M.D. *Vibrational Medicine.* Santa Fe, NM: Bear
& Co., 1988.

Gibran, Kahlil, from http://www.nea-death.com/quotes.html
(accessed October 2007).

Gopnik, Adam. *The King in the Window.* New York:
Hyperion, 2005.

Greenbaum, Norman. "Spirit in the Sky." www.spiritinthesky
.com/. Used with permission of Great Honesty Music.

Greiner, Walter, and Aurel Sandulescu. "New Radioactivities."
Scientific American, March 1990, 58–67.

Halpern, Paul. *The Great Beyond.* Hoboken, NJ: John Wiley &
Sons, 2004.

Hameroff, Stuart, and Roger Penrose. "The Orchestrated
Objective Reduction of Quantum Coherence in Brain
Microtubels: The 'Orch OR' Model for Consciousness."

www.quantumconsciousness.org/penrose-hameroff/orchOR.html
(accessed August 2007).

Hauck, Dennis William. *The Emerald Tablet.* New York:
Penguin, 1999.

Herbert, Brian, and Kevin J. Anderson. *Sandworms of Dune.* New
York: Tor, 2007.

Herbert, Nick, Ph.D. *Faster Than Light: Superluminal Loopholes
in Physics.* New York: Penguin, 1989.

Hoffman, Alice. *The Probable Future.* New York: Random
House, 2003.

Kalweit, Holger. *Dreamtime & Inner Space.* Boston:
Shambhala, 1988.

Karaim, Reed. "Light That Can Cure You." *USA
Weekend,* February 4, 2007. www.usaweekend.com/07_
issues/070204/070204health.html (accessed June 2007).

Kascatan-Nebioglu, Aysegul, Matthew J. Panzner, Claire
A. Tessier, Carolyn L.Cannon, and Wiley J. Youngs.
"N-Heterocyclic Carbene–silver Complexes: A New Class of
Antibiotics." *Coordination Chemistry Reviews* 251, no. 5–6
(2007): 884–895.

Kress, Geraldine J., Kirk E. Dineley, and Ian J. Reynolds. "The
Relationship Between Intracellular Free Iron and Cell Injury in
Cultured Neurons, Astrocytes, and Oligodendrocytes." *Journal
of Neuroscience* 22, no. 14 (2002): 5848–5855.

Langer, W. C. *The Mind of Adolf Hitler: The Secret Wartime
Diaries.* New York: Basic Books, 1972, as referenced in Stevan
J. Thayer and Linda Sue Nathanson, Ph.D., *Interview with an
Angel.* New York: Dell, 1997.

Lipkin, R. "Identifying DNA by the Speed of Electrons (Science News of the Week)," *Science News* 147 (1995): 117.

Livio, Mario. *The Golden Ratio*. New York: Broadway, 2002.

Lloyd, Seth. *Programming the Universe*. New York: Vintage, 2006.

Long, Max Freedom. *The Secret Science Behind Miracles*. Marina del Rey, CA: DeVorss & Company, 1976.

Mails, Thomas E. *Fools Crow: Wisdom and Power*. Tulsa, OK: Council Oak Books, 1991.

McTaggart, Lynne. *The Field*. New York: Harper Perennial, 2002.

Men, Hunbatz. *Secrets of Mayan Science/Religion*. Santa Fe, NM: Bear & Co., 1990.

Morse, M.D., with Paul Perry. *Transformed by the Light*. New York: Villard, 1992.

Newton, Michael, Ph.D. *Journey of Souls*. St. Paul, MN: Llewellyn, 1996.

NIH Website, "Metals in Medicine." www.nigms.nih.gov/news/meetings/metals.html (accessed June 2007).

Oschman, James. *Energy Medicine*. New York: Churchill Livingstone, 2000.

Paterson, David. "Electric Genes: Current Flow in DNA Could Lead to Faster Genetic Testing." *Scientific American,* May 1995, 33–34.

Pearsall, Paul, Ph.D. *The Heart's Code*. New York: Broadway, 1988.

Perkins, John. *The World Is As You Dream It*. Rochester, VT: Destiny Books, 1994.

Pert, Candace B., Ph.D. *Molecules of Emotion*. New York: Scribner, 2003.

Saddhatissa, H. *The Buddha's Way*. New York: George Braziller, 1971.

Schwartz, Gary E., Ph.D., with William L. Simon. *The God Experiments.* New York: Atria Books, 2006.

Shakespeare, William. *Hamlet, Prince of Denmark,* in *The Complete Books of William Shakespeare.* New York: Crown, 1975.

Sheldrake, Rupert. *A New Science of Life.* Rochester, VT: Park Street Press, 1995.

Smith, William, L.L.D. *Smith's Bible Dictionary,* 1868 revised edition. Nashville, TN: Thomas Nelson, 2004.

Somé, Malidoma Patrice. *Of Water and the Spirit.* New York: Penguin, 1994.

Strassman, Rick, M.D. *DMT: The Spirit Molecule.* Rochester, VT: Park Street Press, 2001.

Talbot, Michael. *The Holographic Universe.* New York: HarperCollins, 1991.

Terhart, Franjo. *Beyond Death: Life in the Hereafter.* Bath, UK: Parragon Publishing, 2007.

Thomson, A. J. "The Mechanism of Action of Anti-tumour Platinum Compounds." *Platinum Metals Review* 21, no. 1 (1977): 2–15.

Van Praagh, James. *Talking to Heaven.* New York: Signet, 1999.

Von Bibra, Baron Ernst. *Plant Intoxicants.* Rochester, VT: Healing Arts Press, 1995.

Waters, Frank. *Book of the Hopi.* New York: Ballantine, 1969.

Webb, Stephen. *Out of This World.* New York: Praxix Publishing, in association with Copernicus Books, 2004.

Webster, Richard. *Spirit Guides & Angel Guardians.* St. Paul, MN: Llewellyn, 1998.

Whitton, Joel L., and Joe Fisher. *Life Between Life.* New York: Doubleday, 1986.

Wilbert, Johannes. *Mystic Endowment: Religious Ethnography of the Warao Indians.* Cambridge, MA: Harvard University Press, 1993.

Winkler, Gershon. *Magic of the Ordinary.* Berkeley, CA: North Atlantic, 2003.

Wolf, Fred Alan. *Taking the Quantum Leap.* New York: Harper & Row, 1989.

Wolf, Rabbi Laibl. *Practical Kabbalah.* New York: Three Rivers, 1999.

Yam, Philip. "Bringing Schrödinger's Cat to Life." *Scientific American,* June 1997, 124–129.

Yamada, Tadanori, Yawushi Iwasaki, Hiroko Tada, Hidehiko Iwabuki, Marinee K. L. Chuah, Thierry VandenDriessche, Hideki Fukuda, Akihiko Kondo, Masakazu Ueda, Masaharu Seno, Katsuyuki Tanazawa, and Shun'ichi Kuroda. "Nanoparticles for the Delivery of Genes and Drugs to Human Hepatocytes." *Nature,* August 2003, 885–890, published online at www.nature.com/cgi-taf/DynaPage.taf...abs/nbt843 .html (accessed August 2007).

Ywahoo, Dhyani. *Voices of Our Ancestors: Cherokee Teachings from the Wisdom Fires.* Boston: Shambhala, 1987.

Zukav, Gary. *The Seat of the Soul.* New York: Fireside, 1990.

Web Sites Accessed for Research

www.absolutefact.com/Element_Silver_Facts.html (accessed July 2007).

http://ajpheart.physiology.org/cgi/content/full/282/5/ H1821?ck=nck (accessed July 2007).

www.alchemicals.com/alchemy/ormus-is-a-hydride/686/ (accessed September 2007).

www.altheahayton.com/wombtwin/articles/caseofthevanishi.html (accessed May 2007).

www.answers.com/topic/transition-metal (accessed May 2007).

www.antonine-education.co.uk/Physics_A2/Module_4/Topic_5/ topic_5.htm (accessed May 2007).

www.awakening-healing.com/White%20Powder%20Primer.htm (accessed May 2007).

www.biomedcentral.com/1471-2148/7/S2/S2 (accessed August 2007).

www.chemicalelements.com/groups/transition.htm (accessed May 2007).

www.chemsoc.org/exemplarchem/entries/igrant/uses_noflash .html (accessed May 2007).

www.cocoonnutrition.org/catalog/page_inter_min_NL.php (accessed August 2007).

www.colorado.edu/physics/2000/periodic_table/transition_ elements.html (accessed May 2007).

www.cord.edu/dept/physics/p128/lecture99_34.html (accessed June 2007).

www.daviddarling.info/encyclopedia/M/montmorillonite.html (accessed July 2007).

www.eytonsearth.org (accessed July 2007).

http://ffden-2.phys.uaf.edu/212_fall2003.web.dir/Rodney_ Guritz%20Folder/uses.htm (accessed June 2007).

www.firethegrid.org/eng/home-fr-eng.htm (accessed July 2007).

http://forum.lef.org/default.aspx?f=38&m=16523 (accessed August 2007).

www.freepatentsonline.com/20070009586.html (accessed September 2007).

www.glacialclay.com/aboutus.htm (accessed August 2007).

www.glenbrook.k12.il.us/gbssci/phys/mmedia/waves/swf.html (accessed August 2007).

www.halexandria.org/dward466.htm (accessed May 2007).

http://health.ninemsn.com.au/article.aspx?id=266986 (accessed August 2007).

http://hyperphysics.phy-astr.gsu.edu/hbase/solids/supcon.html (accessed September 2007).

http://id.mind.net/~zona/mstm/physics/waves/standingWaves/ standingWaves.html (accessed June 2007).

www.innovationsgesellschaft.ch/images/publikationen/ Newsletter%20Juni%202007%20Englisch.pdf (accessed September 2007).

www.irondisorders.org/Disorders/about.asp (accessed August 2007).

www.jegem.com/1/healingStones.aspx (accessed July 2007).

www.jewelrysupplier.com/2_copper/copper_healing.htm (accessed September 2007).

www.kettering.edu/~drussell/Demos/superposition/ superposition.html (accessed August 2007).

www.lanl.gov/orgs/mpa/stc/train.shtml (accessed June 2007).

http://lib.bioinfo.pl/meid:205266 (accessed August 2007).

http://linkinghub.elsevier.com/retrieve/pii/S001085450600258X (accessed August 2007).

http://linkinghub.elsevier.com/retrieve/pii/S0169433204007342 (accessed September 2007).

www.medical-library.org/journals_6a/twins_epidemiology.html (accessed August 2007).

www.mrs.org/s_mrs/binasp?CID=2574&DID=59954&DOC=F ILE.PDF (accessed September 2007).

http://newton.dep.anl.give/archieve.html (accessed June 2007).

http://ohioline.osu.edu/hyg-Fact/5000/5559.html (accessed June 2007).

www.patentstorm.us/patents/5382431-claims.html (accessed September 2007).

www.patentstorm.us/patents/5480975-description.html (accessed September 2007).

http://periodic.lanl.gov/elements/76.html (accessed May 2007).

www.pubmedcentral.nih.gov/articlerender.fcgi?artid=45819 (accessed September 2007).

http://sambali.blogspot.com/2006/09/clay-myths-and-uses-of-glossary.html (accessed September 2007).

http://silver-lightning.com/research.html (accessed July 2007).

www.springerlink.com/index/p3uq427k86710657.pdf (accessed September 2007).

www.springerlink.com/index/TL45R736713RM042.pdf (accessed September 2007).

www.subtleenergies.com/ormus/research/research.htm(accessed May 2007).

www.theaethergroup.com/catalog/iridiumrhodium-p-3.html (accessed August 2007).

www.thecdi.com/cobalt-patents-list-LIFE+SCIENCES (accessed September 2007).

www.webelements.com/webelements/elements/text/Rh/key.html (accessed May 2007).

http://en.wikipedia.org/wiki/Cobalt (accessed June 2007).

http://en.wikipedia.org/wiki/Copper (accessed June 2007).

http://en.wikipedia.org/wiki/Copper_healing (accessed September 2007).

http://en.wikipedia.org/wiki/Iridium (accessed June 2007).

http://en.wikipedia.org/wiki/Iron (accessed June 2007).

http://en.wikipedia.org/wiki/Maglev_train (accessed May 2007).

http://en.wikipedia.org/wiki/Mercury (accessed June 2007).

http://en.wikipedia.org/wiki/Montmorillonite (accessed June 2007).

http://en.wikipedia.org/wiki/Osmium (accessed June 2007).

http://en.wikipedia.org/wiki/Palladium (accessed June 2007).

http://en.wikipedia.org/wiki/Palladium_(mytholology) (accessed June 2007).

http://en.wikipedia.org/wiki/Platinum (accessed June 2007).

http://en.wikipedia.org/wiki/Rhodium (accessed June 2007).

http://en.wikipedia.org/wiki/Silver (accessed June 2007).

http://en.wikipedia.org/wiki/Silver_chloride (accessed September 2007).

http://en.wikipedia.org/wiki/Superconductivity (accessed May 2007).

http://en.wikipedia.org/wiki/Transition_metal (accessed May 2007).

http://doi.wiley.com/10.1002/pola.21177 (accessed August 2007).

http://womens-health.health-cares.net/pregnancy-twins.php (accessed August 2007).

http://zptech.net/rhodiridcopdetails.html (accessed September 2007).

Recommended Reading

For further information on transitional metals, superconductivity, and related matters, see the following.

Arai, K. I., W. Sugawara, K. Ishiyama, T. Honda, and M. Yamaguchi. "Fabrication of Small Flying Machines Using Magnetic Thin Films." *IEEE Transactions on Magnetics* 31 (1995): 3758–3760.

Beyond Electrons in a Box: Nanoparticles of Silver, Platinum, and Rhodium. www.springerlink.com/index/p3uq427k86710657.pdf

Biondi, Elisa, Sergio Branciamore, Marie-Christine Marel, and Enzo Gallori. "Montmorillonite Protection of an UV-Irradiated Hairpin Ribozyme: Evolution of the RNA World in a Mineral Environment." *BMC Evolutionary Biology* 2007, 7 (Suppl 2):S2doi:10.1186/1471-2148-7-S2-S2.

Brainard, J. "Ultrasound Prevents Blood Loss in Surgery." *Science News* 153 (1998): 407.

Clark, Richard A. F. "Chapter 46. Wound Repair: Lessons for Tissue Engineering," in Robert P. Lanza, Robert Langer, William L. Chick, eds., *Principles of Tissue Engineering.* Georgetown, TX: R. G. Landes Company, 1997, 737–768.

Duncan, Michael A., and Dennis H. Rouvray. "Microclusters." *Scientific American,* December 1989, 110–115.

Englert, Berthold-Georg, Marlan O. Scully, and Herbert Walther. "The Duality in Matter and Light." *Scientific American,* December 1994, 86–92.

Greiner, Walter, and J. Hamilton. "Is the Vacuum Really Empty?" *American Scientist* 68, no. 2 (1980): 154–164.

Greiner, Walter, G. Soff, and J. Reinhardt. "Spin Polarization of Electrons Induced by Strong Collisional Magnetic Field," *Physics Review* A23 (1981): 701.

Haisch, B., A. Rueda, and H. E. Puthoff. "Beyond E = mc². " *The Sciences* (NY Acadamy of Sciences) 34 (Nov/Dec 1994): 26.

Hirokawa, Nobutaka. "Kinesin and Dynein Superfamily Proteins and the Mechanism of Organelle Transport." *Science* 279 (January 1998): 519–526.

Horgan, John. "Quantum Philosophy." *Scientific American,* July 1992, 94–104.

Horridge, G. A. "The Flight of Very Small Insects." *Nature* 178 (1956): 1334–1335.

Horwitz, Alan F. "Integrins and Health." *Scientific American,* May 1997, 68–75.

Jones, David A., C. Wayne Smith, and Larry V. McIntire. "Leucocyte Adhesion Under Flow Conditions: Principles Important in Tissue Engineering." *Biomaterials* 17 (1996): 337–347.

Koshland, D. E., T. J. Mitchison, and M. W. Kirschner. "Polewards Chromosome Movement Driven by Microtubule Depolymerization in Vitro." *Nature* 331 (1988): 255–318.

Lamond, Angus I., and William C. Earnshaw. "Structure and Function in the Nucleus." *Science* 280 (April 1998): 547–553.

Lawrence, M. B., and T. A. Springer. "Leukocytes Roll on a Selectin at Physiologic Flow Rates: Distinction from and Prerequisite for Adhesion through Integrins." *Cell* 65 (1991): 859–873.

Lighthill, M. J. "On the Weis-Fogh Mechanism of Lift Generation." *Journal of Fluid Mechanics* 60 (August 1973): 1–17.

Macchiavelli, A. O., J. Burde, R. M. Diamond, C. W. Beausang, M. A. Deleplanque, R. J. McDonald, F. S. Stephens, and J. E.

Draper. "Superdeformation" in 104, 105Pd. *Physical Review C* 38, no. 2 (1988): 1088–1091.

Mooney, D., L. Hansen, J. P. Vacanti, et al. "Switching from Differentiation to Growth in Hepatocytes: Control by Extracellular Matrix." *Journal of Cell Physiolology* 151 (1992): 497–505.

Morrison, Philip. "Double Bass Redoubled." *Scientific American,* May 1998, 109–111.

Puthoff, H. E. "CIA-initiated Remote Viewing Program at Stanford Research Institute." *Journal of Scientific Exploration* 10 (1996): 63–76.

———. "Gravity as a Zero-Point-Fluctuation Force." *Physical Review A* 47 (1993): 3454.

———. "Ground State of Hydrogen as a Zero-Point-Fluctuation-Determined State." *Physical Review D* 35 (1987): 3266.

———. "On the Source of Vacuum Electromagnetic Zero-Point Energy." *Physical Review A* 40 (1989): 4857; Errata and Comments, *Phys. Rev. A* 44 (1991): 3382, 3385.

———. "Zero-Point Energy: An Introduction." *Fusion Facts* 3, no. 3 (1991): 1.

Puthoff, H. E., R. Targ, and E. C. May. "Experimental Psi Research: Implications for Physics." In R. G. Jahn, ed., *The Role of Consciousness in the Physical World.* Boulder, CO: Westview, 1981.

Randeria, Mohit, Ji-Min Duan, and Lih-Yir Shieh. "Low-Frequency Relaxation in Ising Spin-Glasses." *Physical Review Letters* 62, no. 9 (1989): 981–984.

Roskelly, C. D., P. Y. Desprez, and M. J. Bissell. "Extracellular Matrix-Dependent Tissue-Specific Gene Expression in

Mammary Epithelial Cells Requires Both Physical and Biochemical Signal Transduction." *Proceedings of the National Academy of Sciences* (USA) 91 (1994): 12378–12382.

Rouhi, A. Maureen. "Nanotechnology—from the ACS Meeting." *Chemical and Engineering News* (April 1998): 57–62.

Shimizu, Y. R. and R. A. Broglia. "Quantum Size Effects in Rapidly Rotating Nuclei." *Physical Review C* 41, no. 4 (1990): 1865–1867.

Shimizu, Y. R., E. Vigezzi, and R. A. Broglia. "Inertias of Super-deformed Bands." *Physical Review C* 41, no. 4 (1990): 1861–1863.

Singhvi, R., A. Kumar, G. Lopez, et al. "Engineering Cell Shape and Function." *Science* 264 (1994): 696–698.

"Star Wars Technology Targets Tumors." *BMDO Update* (Spring 1998): 10.

Steinhardt, Richard A., Guoquiang Bi, and Janet M. Alderton. "Cell Membrane Resealing by a Vesicular Mechanism Similar to Neurotransmitter Release." *Science* 263 (1994): 390–393.

Targ, R., and H. E. Puthoff. *Mind Reach*. New York: Delacorte, 1977.

Tart, C.T., H. E. Puthoff, and R. Targ, eds. *Mind at Large: IEEE Symposia on the Nature of Extrasensory Perception*. New York: Praeger Special Studies, 1979.

Tomb, Howard, and Dennis Kunkel. *MicroAliens: Dazzling Journeys with an Electron Microscope*. New York: Farrar, Straus and Giroux, 1993.

Travis, John. "Stepping Out with Kinesin." *Science* 261 (August 1993): 1112–13.

Tryon, Edward. "Is the Universe a Vacuum Fluctuation?" *Nature* 246 (December 1973): 396–97.

Weis-Fogh, Torkel. "Energetics of Hovering Flight in Hummingbirds and Drosophila." *Journal of Experimental Biology* 56 (1972): 79–104.

———. "Unusual Mechanisms for the Generation of Lift in Flying Animals." *Scientific American,* November 1975, 81–87.

Zhang, Q. M., Vivek Bharti, and X. Zhao. "Giant Electrostriction and Relaxor Ferroelectric Behavior in Electron-Irradiated Poly (vinylidene fluoride-trifluoroethylene) Copolymer." *Science* 280 (June 1998): 2101–2104.

INDEX

ABOUT THE AUTHOR

Cyndi Dale is the author of *New Chakra Healing,* which has been published in more than ten languages, and five other best-selling books on energy healing, including *Advanced Chakra Healing.* Through her company, Essential Energies, she provides intuitive assessments and life-issues healing for thousands of individuals and organizations a year. She especially enjoys helping people awaken their spiritual gifts and destinies, keys to living openhearted and rich lives. Her vitality and wisdom enhance her popular workshops, which she leads around the world. She has created several DVD and CD trainings, including *Advanced Chakra Wisdom* and *Illuminating the Afterlife* through Sounds True. Cyndi has studied cross-cultural healing and led instructional classes in several countries including Peru, Belize, Costa Rica, Japan, Iceland, Russia, Venezuela, Mexico, Morocco, and across Europe. She currently lives in Minneapolis, Minnesota, with her two sons and five pets (at last count). More information on Cyndi's products, seminars, and services is available at www.cyndidale.com.

ABOUT SOUNDS TRUE

Sounds True is a multimedia publisher whose mission is to inspire and support personal transformation and spiritual awakening. Founded in 1985 and located in Boulder, Colorado, we work with many of the leading spiritual teachers, thinkers, healers, and visionary artists of our time. We strive with every title to preserve the essential "living wisdom" of the author or artist. It is our goal to create products that not only provide information to a reader or listener, but that also embody the quality of a wisdom transmission.

For those seeking genuine transformation, Sounds True is your trusted partner. At SoundsTrue.com you will find a wealth of free resources to support your journey, including exclusive weekly audio interviews, free downloads, interactive learning tools, and other special savings on all our titles.

To learn more, please visit SoundsTrue.com/bonus/free_gifts or call us toll free at 800-333-9185.